ADAPT

10 DISRUPTIVE BUSINESS STORIES
100 CONSTRUCTIVE QUESTIONS

ADAPT

TO THRIVE, NOT JUST SURVIVE

HARIT NAGPAL

First published by Westland Business, an imprint of Westland Books, a division of Nasadiya Technologies Private Limited, in 2024

No. 269/2B, First Floor, 'Irai Arul', Vimalraj Street, Nethaji Nagar, Alapakkam Main Road, Maduravoyal, Chennai 600095

ISBN: 9789360452612

10 9 8 7 6 5 4 3 2

Typeset by SŪRYA, New Delhi

Printed at Parksons Graphics Pvt. Ltd

CONTENTS

INTRODUCTION

I have often looked back at my four decades of work across six industries, navigating ever-changing circumstances—working first without computers and then eventually using the internet, email, Google, and now AI. Many times over, I have wondered what has kept me from becoming obsolete. Perhaps my generation's ability to cross-synthesise the fundamentals of business with hands-on experience, without getting daunted by the pace of change around us, kept us going and growing.

To cut a long story short, we adapted. And that is how we survived.

Adaptation in the natural world is best exemplified in the chameleon, which is the reason behind the cover image. The chameleon's adaptive skills are directed towards survival—it becomes almost invisible on any surface it settles on, thus protecting itself from predators. Like the chameleon, humans are capable of adapting themselves—and not just for survival. We adapt also to thrive.

Traditionally, business processes have focused on identifying customer segments they would like to serve, listening to the voice of their customers to create compelling propositions, design services that would fail less often—despite their increasing complexity—and recover quickly in the event of a failure. They made sure their products were easily accessible, and they built brands that touched their customers' hearts and minds.

Are the basic principles of business any different from what they would have been a century ago? Perhaps not. But the environment has been changing, and successful businesses have been adapting to the ever-changing circumstances while operating within the guardrails of these basic principles.

Employees have not changed either, at their core, despite marketers' attempts to assign names to generations beginning with the letters X, Y and Z. People still get a dopamine rush when faced with ambitious goals and challenges. They still prefer to work in silos, and it still takes effort to get them to work in tribes and squads. Hiring and retaining competent people continue to be difficult and making them think out of the box remains a challenge.

With this book, my aim was to explore the basic principles of business as well as the core needs of employees that need to be met if a business is to be truly successful. I wanted to illustrate these principles with my learnings on how businesses can include 'adaptation' in their strategy. The obvious thing to do would have been to build a two-by-two framework for each basic principle and write five thousand words to explain it. But that would have ended up as a textbook my friends and family would have bought but never read.

Most people are sceptical of preachers. Our predecessors were aware of this and masked their teachings in tales we call mythology. Today, mothers ensure their children receive the nutrition of bland milk by masking it with chocolate. It is the chocolate that makes children open their mouths for the milk, which they may not have accepted otherwise. Stories are like chocolate. They help open our minds and absorb lessons from others' experiences. If heard repeatedly, these learnings become internalised, like calcium from the milk strengthening the child's teeth and bones.

This idea of the importance of storytelling was playing on my mind when I began work on the book. I took up each subject and created a situation around it, as close as possible to real life, to help explain the process of adaptation. Most of the stories here are based on what I saw or experienced. I have myself lived three of the ten stories, nuances and all, and those who know me can figure out which these stories are.

I also set these stories in different countries and industries—even on a different world—just to make the point that genius as well as stupidity are universal. Some of these countries and industries I have never been a part of. Researching them was the best part of writing the book, and I learnt a lot in the process.

To articulate the key messages and with the hope that the learning would be absorbed, I have added ten questions at the end of each story. These questions need to be answered with a 'yes' or a 'no', without the option of adding an 'if' or a 'but'. The 'if' and the 'but', followed by a justification, are barriers that come in the way of learning and of progress. I would urge the reader to probe deeper into the questions to which they responded with a 'no' by researching on the internet or speaking with experts.

I enjoyed writing this book. It made me aware that even after four decades, there is a great deal still for me to learn and to adapt to, and that there are pages of the book of business that I have not yet turned. If it leaves you with the same feeling, my effort will have been rewarded.

1

THE CUSTOMERS WE WANT, AND THOSE WE DON'T WANT

Navigating targeted segments

Sam is the global CEO of a consumer products company headquartered in New York. His company has recently acquired a loss-making brand, Wallah, in Bangladesh. This is Sam's first visit to Dhaka to meet the senior team of Wallah to figure out a direction for the future.

Sam last visited Bangladesh two decades ago, when he went to wind up his parents' home in Dhaka and take them to his new home in the outskirts of New York—a home he had bought after fifteen years of first studying and then working in the US. Those fifteen years in the US had changed many things in his life, including his name from Shamsuddin to Sam.

As he sits in the back seat of the Rolls Royce Phantom sent to the airport by his childhood friend Mujib, it dawns on Sam that even though in the last two decades much has changed in Dhaka, a lot has remained the same. The city has a new airport with aerobridges, escalators and backlit signages and yet, before he could exit the airport, he had to fill up many immigration forms and go through multiple manual security checks, practices reminiscent of days gone by. On his drive from the airport, he encounters several new flyovers and underpasses, but those don't seem to have made a difference to the traffic—the mix of haphazardly driven two- and four-wheelers still moves as slowly as before. Most road crossings have traffic lights that are working properly, and yet he can see traffic cops superseding those lights and guiding the traffic manually, thus causing jams. Pedestrians are walking freely between slow-moving cars, and from the corner of his eye he can see a goat trying to cross the busy street. On the way to Mujib's house in Gulshan, a posh residential locality where his relatives and friends are gathering to welcome him, he sees slums, people sitting by the footpath staring into space and many other signs of underemployment and unemployment. Seeing all this, he wonders whether his company made the right decision when it invested in Wallah.

To kill time, Sam strikes up a conversation with Kazi, Mujib's driver.

'Kazi, how long have you worked with Mujib?'

'Thirty-five years, sir.'

'You've been driving for Mujib for thirty-five years?' asks Sam, astonished.

'I started as a helper with Mujib sir's father in their old

house. You may not recall, but I remember you came to meet him with Mujib sir when you were both young boys. It was Mujib sir who taught me how to drive and I've been driving his car for twenty years now.'

'And do you live in the house with them?'

'I live near Dhanmondi, which is not far away. Mujib sir bought me a Bajaj bike. It takes me only thirty-five to forty minutes to reach home now,' says Kazi.

'Do drivers make good money in Bangladesh?'

'A young driver can make around 12,000 taka a month.'

'Hmm, that would be about 150 dollars …' muses Sam.

'If you say so, sir. Since I've worked with Mujib sir for a long time and he trusts me with his personal tasks, he gives me 22,000 taka.'

'Who else is there in your family?' asks Sam.

'I have a wife who works in a garment factory. She started as a packer, but over the years she has moved up the ranks and is now a storekeeper. We have two sons—one is twenty-seven and the other is twenty-four. The elder one did well in his studies, so he's got a pensionable government job. The younger wasn't very good at school; he was always playing cricket. So, Mujib sir gave him a job in one of his factories in Noakhali. Now he stays there full-time and comes home once a month.'

'So, the family is settled. Good.'

'*Alhamdulillah*! Allah has been kind. Both Sabiha, my wife, and I worked hard to make sure that the boys didn't have to struggle like we've had to. We live in a rented home right now but we can hope that one day the boys will buy their own homes and look after us when we become old,' says Kazi with a sigh.

The conversation makes the ten-kilometre drive seem shorter than it is. Despite driving through peak traffic, they roll into Mujib's home within thirty minutes of leaving the airport.

One glimpse inside Mujib's home and Sam feels as if he is no longer in Bangladesh. The interiors of the house—the flooring, the chandeliers, the furniture, the art—as well as the way everyone is dressed give Sam the sense of being in a rich Western European home. The coexistence of Mujib's and Kazi's worlds, so close to each other yet so different, is intriguing. Clearly, the country has progressed a lot since he left over three decades ago, but it has done so selectively.

Mujib gives Sam a welcoming hug as he walks into the family lounge. While they wait for Mujib's wife, Najma, who is still getting ready for the evening, they are joined by Mujib's son, Zia.

Mujib and Najma have visited Sam in the US often, more frequently when Zia was studying at Princeton. And, at least once a month, Zia would come over to Sam's place, even staying over a few times.

Five years ago, on his return from Princeton, Zia had noticed that unlike the US, Bangladesh did not have too many ready-to-cook food options. During his college days, Zia had always had a well-stocked freezer full of ready-to-cook meal packs, which he replenished once a week from a supermarket.

In contrast, the supermarket near his Dhaka home sold only fresh meats and vegetables, which required long hours of preparation and cooking. When probed, Zia's friends who had also studied abroad echoed his observation that there was a huge opportunity for ready-to-cook meals in the market, especially given the rising numbers of millennials who, despite having help at home, preferred to do things by themselves.

Zia teamed up with a school friend, Alam, and the two started working on a project to seize what they felt was a nascent yet promising opportunity. They spent three months in the US, meeting people of Asian origin who lived there and were regular consumers of ready-to-cook frozen foods. They conducted research on the most popular brands of frozen food amongst Asians and the kind of seasonings they preferred. They discovered that most Asians were buying ready-to-cook foods because it was convenient, but were also embellishing them with spices which they brought whole from their home countries and ground at home, because they found Western flavours too bland for their palate.

While in the US, Zia and Alam had also met executives of companies producing some of the most popular ready-to-cook brands. They were all very keen to venture into a highly populated market like Bangladesh, especially with an enthusiastic local partner who could help them overcome any hurdles arising from local trade and government policies.

In three months, Zia and Alam had managed to tick off all the boxes that they thought were necessary to start their venture. They knew the flavours they wanted to launch with and had signed a licensing arrangement with one of the largest frozen foods brands in the US.

On their return, Zia and Alam formed a company and named their brand Shaad, which means relish in Bangla. They retained majority ownership of the company for themselves, with the US firm as their minority partner, in line with local government regulations. To start the company, the boys obtained funding from their fathers, and bridged the gap in funding with debt from a bank whose chairman was a close friend of their families. They applied for government permissions, picked a site for the plant, created a cold chain with ten refrigerated trucks to distribute the product and hired seventy-five people, mainly for the manufacturing and sales functions.

This is the last update Sam has about Zia's business. Two years ago, when Zia came to New York to meet his partners, he stayed with Sam. Sam vividly remembers a conversation they had during that visit.

'Zia, who do you think your customer is?' Sam asked.

'Anyone who's hungry, is short on time, or lazy. It could be a homemaker who's not in the mood to do the cutting and chopping that day, someone who's had a long tiring day at work and wants to spend the evening relaxing rather than prepping for dinner, a youngster who's hungry after a late-night party but doesn't want to wake anyone else up to cook for them—it could be almost anyone.'

'Are you just guessing, or is this what a formal market segmentation study has told you?'

'Do we really need to spend time, effort and money on a segmentation study when the need is so clear and obvious?' Zia asked.

'Maybe you do. You see, income, buying power and cultural influences are not the same across different customer segments, that is, the housewives, working women and party-going youngsters you've just mentioned as your potential customers. These factors vary even more across culturally and economically different countries.'

'But you do agree that all these segments are potential consumers who are waiting for something like this to be launched, don't you?'

'Maybe. However, I am not sure how *many* of the housewives, working women and partying millennials that you have in mind would be inclined to buy your products, or how often they would buy them, or what the best price would be to appeal to them. That is what a segmentation study can tell you.'

'Alam and I checked the carts of shoppers at Target and other grocery stores every day for the three months that we were in the US and we saw all these customer segments buy ready-to-cook frozen foods in large quantities.'

'I'm not sure if an anecdotal and limited sample survey, carried out only in a few US cities, can be representative of what a customer in Bangladesh might want. Compared to the large investment you guys are making in setting up your plant, the cost of a segmentation study would be peanuts,' Sam argued.

'It would just delay the project and someone else could seize the opportunity before we do.'

'I'd rather have someone else make the mistake because they're in a hurry rather than you. A business needs to be sure of the customers it wants to target, and even more importantly, those it does not want to target.'

'Why would a business not want to target customers who are willing to buy its products?' asked Zia.

'It's not necessary for your brand to target every customer who is willing to buy your product. Some customers might be interested in buying, but they may want to pay a price that is lower than what the brand can afford to sell at. Some potential customers could be living at a distance from the place where the product is being manufactured; the transportation cost incurred in making sure your product reaches them could wipe out your margins. Some customers might only want to buy your products on certain occasions; you will have to spend a lot of money on advertising to stay on top of mind so they remember to buy your product when that occasion arrives.'

'How can we know all this without investing in manufacturing, marketing and sales, without taking the product to the customers and seeing their response?' Zia asked.

'Doing all that first would be too expensive and could wipe out your entire capital. In contrast, a relatively inexpensive segmentation study could tell you how large each customer segment is, whether these segments are living in a few geographies or are scattered all over the place, the cost of getting the product to them based on their location, how often they are likely to buy your product and how much they are likely to buy each time, what price they would like to pay, what feature of your product appeals to them the most. All this information will help you to understand what your main proposition should be while advertising, what medium you should use to get your message to them and other important factors to consider while marketing and advertising your products. I could just go on and on.'

'Sounds interesting. This is stuff they taught us in college. I wonder if there's a place for it in real life though?' Zia said.

There was one more conversation that Sam had had with Zia during that visit about the buying preferences of customers.

'Would you say that a homemaker would spend less when cooking for her family than when entertaining guests?' he asked Zia.

'That's likely.'

'You know, our daughter Samira checks out multiple stores before she buys a ten-dollar T-shirt. Yet, the same Samira walks into the showroom of a designer she trusts and walks out, within minutes, with a 3,000-dollar dress she wants to wear to a friend's wedding.'

'I'd do the same too.'

'Now take my case. While going on a work trip, I usually choose an airline that might be expensive but provides direct connections, has a better record on punctuality and offers the service of a lounge if there is a layover. However, for a family vacation I tend to pick an airline with a lower fare, even if it has stopovers or occasionally gets delayed.'

'Dad does the same too. He made us travel economy for our Vietnam holiday last year, while he and Mom travelled business class.'

'That brings me to my question—do you want your product to play in the ten-dollar, low-margin, high-volume T-shirt segment or would you prefer to target the limited-volume, high-price and high-margin designer dress segment? The answer to this question will help you tailor your product as well as streamline your strategy for communication, distribution, investments, and other costs and margins.'

'Right now, we've decided to launch it at a price that will make us some money, leaving it to the customers to decide the occasion they want to use our products for.'

'Zia, you're reminding me of the time when I was briefly posted in Egypt to head our company's business there. My team would often come to me with products aimed at the premium segment. However, what I usually saw while sitting in my expensive car, driving from my luxury hotel near the pyramids to our office in the posh city centre, told me that most people in Egypt lived very differently from people like us. That's why I would keep sending back the proposals my team sent me, and insisted that they came up with products that the masses could afford. I think the business in Egypt survived and grew because of my repeated pushbacks in those early years. And now, my gut tells me that the income skews in Bangladesh must be more like in Egypt and less like in the

US. Bangladesh probably has a few affluent homes with not enough time and a lot of money on their hands. In contrast, there may be a very large segment of underemployed people who have a lot of free time but not enough money at their disposal.'

'But the impoverished won't buy ready-to-cook food. They wouldn't see any value in spending money on it,' Zia argued.

'Exactly my point. But think about this too. Those who are economically affluent probably have enough help at home to cook for them and can have anything they wish to eat, which means they, too, may not find any value in ready-to-cook food.'

'But we've already got the necessary funding and a partnership agreement with the largest frozen-foods brand in the US. We can't abandon the project at this stage.'

'Maybe you should, if the segmentation study tells you to do that. Or, maybe you can aim to target only a specific segment that would be profitable and discard the unprofitable ones. It may not be a great idea to invest money on an idea that originated in the US and has found acceptance only among a handful of your rich friends in Bangladesh.'

'Hmm.'

'There is another way to do this, to figure out who might buy your products and who most certainly won't. If you can get hold of an income-wise break-up of the population, you can figure out how many people fall into each income bracket. Then take the price of one family-size serving of your product and calculate the number of hours a person in each of these income brackets would have to work to buy that serving. I haven't seen the data, but I can say with some confidence that while most of the American population will need to work for a few minutes to buy one serving, the same serving would require maybe half a day's work for most people living in Bangladesh. Would they spend that kind of money to save only a few minutes of their day? I doubt that very much.'

Sam recalls that while Zia listened to him attentively, his mind seemed to have been already made up. The glint in his eyes told Sam that he couldn't wait to launch the product he was already so much in love with. So he decided not to burden him with any more anecdotes from his own experience and wished him luck.

Two years after that conversation, Sam settles down with a cup of black coffee to talk to Zia. He hopes to get an update on the business venture before their dinner guests begin to arrive.

Zia is looking less enthusiastic than Sam remembers and is making limited eye contact while they talk.

'So, tell me, what happened with Shaad?' asks Sam.

'Well, we had a big launch for the brand. A friend of Dad's, who is a government official here, was the chief guest. We took on a young and hip youth icon as our brand ambassador and bought enough media ads to dominate the front page of every newspaper and the back page of every magazine. We paid social media influencers to post good reviews. We also rented prime space in all supermarkets in upmarket Dhaka and got ourselves listed on every food delivery app in Dhaka. We figured that most large grocery stores would either have small freezers or no freezers at all, so we invested in freezers as well and placed them with our branding prominently in these stores.'

'Wow, you pulled out all the possible stops. All that must have led to a huge offtake for your product.'

'Yes, we didn't leave anything to chance. In the first two weeks, while the advertising was on, the sales were great. We would often run out of our products in stores and on occasion, Dad had to send his personal cars to help deliver the products and plug the gaps. At the end of the week, we hosted a party to celebrate the launch, and it was attended by the who's who of the country.'

'Wow! All this sounds fantastic!'

'But it didn't last. As soon as the aggressive advertising stopped, the sales dropped too. A month later, the demand for our products was so low that it could be fulfilled by running the factory for just one day in a week.'

'So, what did you do after that?'

'How to make sales pick up was the only subject that was discussed at home for more than a week. One evening, over dinner, Mom came up with a brilliant insight. She felt that maybe customers were not buying Shaad because they didn't know what it would taste like. She thought that the product required sampling, at scale.'

'That's logical. Your mom has always been the wise one in the family,' says Sam, tongue-in-cheek.

'I checked with Alam, and his girlfriend agreed with what Mom was saying. So we set up tasting stations in all the seventeen large stores present in Dhaka. Sales shot up again. The factory started running for three days a week to meet the demand. However, a week after we stopped the trials, sales dipped again, almost to half of what they had been during the trials. That's when our accountant informed us that the money left in the bank was only sufficient to pay one month's salaries to our employees and to refund the instalment of the loan we had taken from the bank.'

'That must have been hard,' sympathises Sam.

'Yes, it was. However, Mom came to our rescue again. She suggested that we create bulk packs which could be used by street-food vendors in Dhaka to cater to their customers. She felt the volume would at least keep our factories running long enough for us to pay our bills.

'We checked with a few vendors and they liked the idea. They suggested that we provide them with new carts, signs and disposable plates and cutlery, all with prominent Shaad branding. Though it was expensive, it seemed like a good way to take the brand to the masses. We hoped that if people liked what the vendors dished up, they would be tempted to buy the products on their next visit to the store.'

'That's a big swing of customer segments, isn't it?' asks Sam.

'It was, but we didn't have too many choices left. We had to keep the factory running in order to pay salaries and meet the demand of the bank loan. So, we decided to cut our advertising budget and divert the funds towards what the vendors were demanding. This shift required fresh funding.

The banks agreed to grant us more loans, provided the shareholders brought in a fresh round of equity. Thankfully, Dad and Alam's father agreed to do that.'

'Did the plan work?'

'Yes and no. Bulk pack sales took off and the factory started running all seven days of the week. Due to the low margins of bulk sales, our profit margin was low, but the cash that came in allowed us to meet our day-to-day working capital needs. Every business paper carried stories and pictures of Alam and me, calling us "Turnround Artistes".'

'Wonderful! You have your mother to thank for the idea, though.'

'And I did, but the boom in sales didn't last very long. Three months later, purchases from the street vendors started to flatten, followed by a sharp decline in sales. Our sales guys initially told us that this was because the stock pipe was cleaning itself after a massive year-end billing. But nothing changed and even after a month, sales didn't pick up.'

'Did you find the cause?'

'Yes. We realised that while we were using fine organic grains as raw material for our products, apparently a product similar to ours but unbranded, made from relatively cheaper grain by housewives in Dhaka's slums, was being supplied in bulk packs to the vendors at half the price of Shaad's. Within two months, most vendors had stopped buying from us, but they continued with our branding, so their customers thought they were eating Shaad instead of a different product with a lower quality.'

'Did you not sue the vendors?'

'Our lawyers recommended that we don't. They felt it wouldn't yield anything substantial since we didn't have written contracts with the vendors.'

'That's sensible advice. I'm sure you didn't want to lose any more money on unnecessary litigation. So, what did you do afterwards?'

'What could we do? We shut down the factory and gave termination notices to all our employees, barring the accounts staff. Dad has initiated the liquidation process for the firm. His relations with the bank and the government are coming in handy to help us recover whatever we can of our investment.'

'I am sorry, Zia. That's really unfortunate. It seems to me that for the factory to run all seven days of the week, you'll need volumes which can come only if you target the mass market and not just the affluent class. Also, the move made by the small-scale guys into your market share makes it clear that your product is liked, albeit at a lower price. Since you've tried so many other options to make the business work, think about giving it one more shot before winding up.'

Sam pauses to gather his thoughts.

'Switch your raw material to something cheaper to bring down the prices. I'm sure you'll be able to beat the cost of the small-scale guys with your production scale. That'll allow you to go back to the vendors at a price equal to, or maybe even lower than, the price at which they're getting the other product now. And, if this works out, you can consider selling your products at every neighbourhood provision store instead of premium supermarkets.'

'You think that'll work?' Zia looks hopefully at Sam.

'Worth trying, I'd say. You have nothing to lose.'

The grandfather clock in a corner of the room strikes six. Time to get dressed for dinner. The two men rise and Sam puts his arm around the younger man's shoulders. 'You know, Zia, if there's one thing I've learnt, it's this: a business needs to keep its plans flexible and adapt with every change, quickly.'

At dinner, Sam meets the many old friends Mujib has invited, some of them after almost thirty-five years. There are bankers, lawyers, two politicians, and even a couple of bureaucrats amongst them. In the course of the evening, it becomes apparent to Sam that most of them believe the country's economy is growing fast and that the large population coupled with low wages could help distinguish Bangladesh from other countries, making it a preferred supplier for the West.

Next morning, Sam meets the team of Wallah, the Bangladeshi consumer goods company his firm has acquired. Sitting through the presentations that follow, he finds that the team is passionate and fiercely competitive and has a winner's attitude.

Wallah is a pioneering brand in its category and was the choice of premium customers for almost a decade, when there were only two competitors in the market—Wallah and Wake-Up. A couple of years ago, three other brands had entered the market, with lower-quality products and lower prices. This had led to Wallah losing its entire cash reserves and half its market share in the pyrrhic battles for control that followed. Finally, the company had been left with no option but to sell to Sam's firm for infusion of some fresh equity.

Sam watches Wallah's CEO Taufiq's face beam with joy every time someone from his team makes a statement like, 'We have the highest share of the wholesalers' market', 'We match every competitor's price within four hours flat', 'We do not lose any customer, at any cost, ever', 'We have the most shop signs', 'We release the most ads', 'We sponsor more events than any other brand in Bangladesh' and so on. But he also notices that when it comes to metrics like market share, revenue and profit, the company is a distant third or fourth amongst the five local brands in the same category.

Taufiq sums up the day's discussions by saying, 'Return on investments made in this industry will take a while to come, hence this is not the place for the weakhearted to invest in. Wallah is committed to a high-growth strategy which will require cash burn in the short run. We will make tons of money while other competitors will lose hope and, eventually, only a couple of us will remain in the market.'

Sam smiles and punctuates his smiles with encouraging words. However, the question that remains unanswered in his head is, 'If the people are so driven and the brand is so strong, why did the company run out of funds, only to be sold off later?'

Sam also notices that only the sales and marketing staff are present for this review meeting. When he asks Taufiq about the others, he is told, 'Oh, we thought we were only going to discuss the business.'

Since Sam's return flight is after midnight on the following day, he asks Taufiq if he can visit some Wallah customers during the day. Taufiq agrees and offers to accompany him on the visit.

Next morning, Sam suggests that they take the N3 highway out of the city. He is familiar with the route, having spent many summer vacations in Mymensingh with his grandparents, who passed away while he was in college in the US. He plans to take short stops at Gazipur, Bhaluka and Trishal along the way to meet some customers. It will also give him the chance to grab a meal of fish curry and rice, a taste that still lingers in his memories.

Thirty miles out of the city, they make their first stop. After that they stop every twenty to thirty minutes to meet a customer or wherever they find a cluster of shops. By lunch, they have met at least ten dealers and many more customers.

Sam has observed something strange. While every large store is selling Wallah's products, none of the small shops are. When he asks the small shop owners, they tell him that Wallah's products are too expensive, and that their customers prefer the cheaper products sold by Wallah's competitors. Since no Wallah sales executive has ever visited these small shops, none of the owners is aware that Wallah products are priced the same as the other brands they have been stocking. All the large stores in Dhaka have some Wallah signage or a poster or two, but none is visible in the smaller shops in the city or in any shops once you leave the city and enter the neighbouring towns.

Sam probes Taufiq for the reasons for this when they stop for lunch at Mymensingh.

'Wallah's price is now the same as that of other competing brands. Then why haven't we advertised the new price and made ourselves more visible to customers by advertising in all kinds of shops?'

'Wallah has always been and remains an aspirational brand—a brand meant for premium customers. Dropping prices to match those of our competitors was a necessity. However, we believe that selling at small shops and advertising the lower price aggressively will take away the premium brand value.'

'If that is the case, aren't you losing out on the volume gain opportunity that the price drop was meant to deliver?'

'That may be so. But our premium customers will be upset if they find out that we have started catering to all segments of society. To put it crudely, most of them don't want to feel like they are eating what their drivers are eating.'

On the drive back to Dhaka, Sam is thinking of situations that Zia and Taufiq are trapped in with respect to their customer segments. While Zia, with Shaad, is jumping thoughtlessly from one segment to the other, Taufiq, on the other hand, is holding on to the carefully targeted customer segment he launched Wallah with, even as his customers have moved on and new segments have emerged. He starts a conversation to provoke Taufiq.

'So, what kind of music do you like to listen to, Taufiq?'

'Oh, my taste in music remains the same as when I was younger. I find the new style of music very loud and meaningless.'

'Me too. I remember my parents had this big radio that was later replaced with a battery-charged transistor. You could carry it around everywhere. Then came LPs, cassette tapes, CDs, and now they're all gone. Everything is on this phone, living inside apps. The devices have kept changing over the years, but my taste in music has remained the same.'

'You know, I felt terrible discarding my carefully curated collection of LPs, then cassettes and CDs. But surprisingly, each time I tried to sell something that I thought had become outdated, there was someone who was willing to buy them, at a lower price of course. They must have had a usable player, because why else would they buy those LPs, cassettes and CDs, even if it wasn't for very much money?'

'Yeah, I guess not everyone moves on to new technology as soon as it's introduced. On my last visit to Nigeria, I saw a shop selling transistor radios. And there I was, thinking they had gone extinct!'

'Changes like these are not just limited to music. Look at the travel industry. While air traffic is continuously growing and some affluent people are even using private jets, the crush of people on trains and buses is not reducing,' Taufiq says.

'I guess the affluent class buys into a category first and become early adaptors. But as the product becomes popular and the volume of sales goes up, the scale of production makes the product cheaper, making it affordable even for the masses.'

'And, if at the same time, someone innovates and finds a new and superior technology to fulfil the same need, the affluent class gets a new alternative to adopt.'

'Yes. And this cycle continues. Customer segments are not static, it seems.'

'I guess advertising and distribution channels also need to adapt with the movement in customer segments. They need to talk to, and reach, new customer segments, to convince them to buy products that were once affordable only to the affluent. So, the cassette or CD seller, who was earlier talking to me and trying to get me to buy his products, now needs to target my staff.'

'Exactly right. Do we have someone in the marketing department of Wallah who has prior experience of working with a consumer research firm?' asks Sam.

'We had hired someone with this profile but he left within a year of joining. We've tried to fill the position many times after that. It's difficult to find someone with that background who is willing to join the company and stay beyond a year or two.'

'I faced the same problem when I was our company's CEO for Canada. Finally, I reconciled myself to the fact that people of this profile are difficult to tame. They enjoy working in research firms where they handle multiple product categories simultaneously. Beyond a point, extra money doesn't mean anything to them. If you do manage to hire a good consumer research specialist who agrees to stay on for a couple of years, the cost is well worth it. And if you manage to get someone who enjoys your business environment and sticks around for longer, you are truly blessed.'

It's time now for Sam to head back. He says his goodbyes to Taufiq and thanks him for showing him around.

Back at the hotel, while preparing for another long flight, Sam calls Rick, his global HR partner, and asks him to make a list of the best customer segmentation specialists they employ across all geographies. He also asks him to select one of these specialists, someone who is willing to relocate to a different country for a short while, and send him to Dhaka for three months. The specialist's mandate would be to build a local cross-functional team comprising commercial and finance functions that would be able to track the profitability of each customer segment. This would help Wallah to focus on the customers they want to target and go after them with aggressive advertising and a well-executed distribution plan.

It is clear to Sam that this is the first building block for the turnaround plan of Wallah.

Meanwhile, Taufiq calls his assistant and asks her to set up meetings with his sales, service and marketing heads first thing the following day. He wants to discuss distribution reach enhancement and a new advertising campaign for Wallah products. He also wants a meeting with the HR head to discuss the search for a marketing executive with experience in consumer research.

That night, when Taufiq rests his fountain pen on his bedside table before going to bed, he wonders how long it will be before the humble fountain pen, too, meets the fate of the once ubiquitous cassettes and CDs.

He is sure that someone somewhere is already trying to find a new customer segment for pens and is thinking of a good way to sell pens to that segment.

Here are some statements that you should respond to with respect to the business that you are a part of, as an owner or a manager. Remember to respond honestly.

The statements must be answered in a yes/no format. If there are any statements that are not relevant to your business, put a cross against them.

- ☐ We have broken our industry category into customer segments and we revisit them once a year, to confirm if they still exist and to check if any distinct and sizeable new segments have emerged or are likely to emerge.
- ☐ We have people with prior experience of identifying and building customer segments in other industries.
- ☐ We have identified profitable and growing target segments, from which we acquire and retain customers. We have products that these segments consider affordable and have sales channels in place to reach such segments.

- ☐ We have identified customer segments that we would not want to sell to because they are either too small, too scattered, or the price these segments are willing to pay makes them unprofitable for us.
- ☐ Our target segments are not the same for every major geography and we have a buy-in from the local teams.
- ☐ We have given our target segments 'human' names like 'Affluent Bob', 'Struggling Sandra', 'Overworked Sally', etc., to give them a clear identity. Our non-commercial and sales staff are familiar with these names and can recall the characteristics of the customers in each of these segments.
- ☐ We have tailored our advertising and media strategies for each target segment, based on the attitudes, beliefs and media habits of each target segment, and we probe and update these strategies regularly.
- ☐ We measure the health of a target segment by the net customer additions to the segment and the change in per customer consumption and revenue. This is reviewed quarterly for every significant geography. The performance of our commercial teams is linked to this change.
- ☐ In the last twelve months, we have chosen not to match a competitor's price move at least once, because the customer segment our competitor was targeting did not qualify as a suitable target segment for us.
- ☐ In the last twelve months, we have introduced at least one proposition to attract, retain or grow a new target segment.

Now consider the statements to which you have responded with a 'No'. Discuss and reflect on these within your company, read more about **consumer segmentation**, and/or ask some experts about how to apply these statements to your specific case.

Doing this could prevent your company from going into liquidation or being sold.

2

EARS TO THE GROUND

Listening to the customer

Marco Rossi and Elisabetta grew up in the quaint little town of Bergamo, an hour's drive from Milan. After graduation, Marco got a rookie's job at a publishing firm in Milan. He moved to the city and started living with an aunt.

A year later, after he was confirmed in his job, he rented a place of his own and proposed to Elisabetta on one of his trips back home. After a big wedding in Bergamo, attended by the families and the many friends of the couple, Elisabetta moved to Milan with Marco.

After working with the publishing house for ten years, Marco started a weekly magazine called *Punto di Vista*, and followed it up with an afternoon tabloid of the same name. It became popularly known as *PdV* and Marco was sharp enough to trademark the acronym and change the masthead to the name by which people asked for it at newspaper kiosks.

Business was good, and the circulation of both the magazine and the tabloid grew rapidly over the years. Today, Marco has some of the best names in journalism on his payroll or freelancing for him. The company has over six hundred employees, more than any other newspaper business in Milan.

The last three decades have seen Marco and Elisabetta move home twice, each time for a house larger than the previous one. They have two children—Stella, thirty, is an architect and Stefano, twenty-eight, is a reporter with a local daily.

Stella met a young man called Luca in college. They fell in love and then moved in together. After college, they took up their first assignment at the same architectural firm and eventually started their own firm, which specialised in designing and building large villas. Three years and six villas later, Luca proposed to Stella. Then, late one evening, they come to meet Marco and Elisabetta and tell them that they wish to get married.

Marco and Elisabetta are overjoyed. Elisabetta has been waiting for this day for a long time, dreaming of a large wedding for her daughter in their hometown of Bergamo, with the celebrations spread over several days. That night, after Stella and Luca have left, Elisabetta sends excited messages to her sisters, giving them the good news and asking them to prepare for the big event.

In the morning, just as Elisabetta is sitting down for breakfast, Stella calls her mother.

'Luca and I have decided to call off the wedding,' she says.

'But why? Did you guys have a fight?' Elisabetta asks, horrified.

'No. We didn't fight.'

'Then what happened, my love? You looked so happy together last night.'

'Nothing happened. I am just upset. Very, very upset.'

'But why? What did Luca do to upset you so much?'

'It's not him I am upset with. It's you. Why did you have to go and announce to the whole world that we are getting married without even telling me?'

'The whole world? I just told Sofia and Lisa. They are my sisters, our family,' says Elisabetta, astonished.

'And they told half of Bergamo. All I've done since the morning is answer congratulatory calls.'

'It is a big event, my love. Everyone is excited. It's only natural for them to call and congratulate you. The whole family is so fond of you.'

'And who decided that we will have a big fat wedding? That too in Bergamo?' asks Stella, her voice rising in anger.

'Well, our entire family is in Bergamo. I thought it would be easier for us to go there for the wedding rather than having everyone come down to Milan. It's going to be so much harder making arrangements for so many people to stay in Milan.'

'Mama, it's my wedding and if I'm not allowed to decide how, where and when to get married, then I don't want to have a wedding at all. Bye!' Stella hangs up, having said her piece.

Elisabetta is stunned. She has no idea why Stella is so angry with her for doing something every mother does for her daughter.

It's a big day for Marco. His son, Stefano, after having worked for a couple of years as a reporter in another publishing house, is finally joining the family business as the head of marketing. Marco has got a new cabin made for him and proudly welcomes his son on his first day of work.

Later that day, Marco calls for a review meeting with his senior management team. Stefano is invited too.

'Sales of *PdV* have dropped from ten million to eight million over the last six years and the decline is accelerating with every passing month. We've lost almost a million in the last ten months alone. Even the circulation numbers of the weekly are down to a million versus the two million copies we were selling just two years ago,' Marco begins.

'Everyone's sales are down right now. It's not just us,' says the commercial head.

'So what? I've been running this paper for twenty years and I've seen more winters than any of you guys. This is not the first time that sales of newspapers and magazines have gone down industry-wide. Except, in the past, it was our competitors who got frostbite. We remained unaffected for the most part. Then why are things different this time?'

'This winter has been rather long,' says the circulation head, hoping to placate Marco.

'Don't blame the weather or your circumstances for this. The fault lies within us. When was the last time we were the first to break some big news before our competitors? I can't even recall. That's because we aren't making full use of our contacts. It was the frequent drinking sessions with the boys in the government and the police that allowed us to be the first ones with the news.'

'I met the commissioner last week. He sends you his regards,' the PR head pipes up.

'It's not the commissioner who gets us the leads. They come from local beats, from the constables. Our reporters are not meeting them often enough. And don't even get me started on the writing style. We have started to sound like a school noticeboard. Our copy lacks passion, leave alone fire.'

'We've brought back all the editorial staff we fired six months ago and have let go of the lot we hired then. We can hope to see some improvement soon,' says the HR head.

'That's not enough. I want a list from everyone. A list of people who are sleeping on the job. Not just names. I want you to confirm the date by which they will be out of our office.'

'That's a harsh move, Marco.'

'So are the times, my darling. And I want another list too. A list of the best journalists our competitors have. Let's poach them. Buy them out at any cost. Whatever fancy designation they want, give it to them. I want my last year's subscriber numbers back. Is that clear to everyone or do I have to repeat myself?'

Later in the day, father and son sit down in Marco's room for lunch. Over homemade food, Stefano asks Marco if anyone in the office has met their customers—those who continue to subscribe and those who have cancelled their subscriptions. Maybe people are now getting their news from TV or news apps? Maybe the content and the writing style that used to work earlier have ceased to excite the younger lot? In fact, maybe *PdV* needs to explore the idea of launching an online version of the paper and a TV news channel too.

Marco is angry and offended. 'Did Steve Jobs go around asking phone users what kind of a phone they'd like to use before he launched the iPhone? Could anyone have told him that they wanted an iPhone?' he asks his son, sharply. He reiterates that he has taken the paper from zero to where it is today only by following his nose. 'In the publishing business,' he says, 'either you know what you have to do or you don't; you can't go around asking people what you should do.'

Marco is all riled up by now. He continues, 'The smell of ink on freshly printed paper and the act of opening it page after page can never be replicated by the clicking of links on any phone or news app. TV has been around for many years now. It is watched by twice the number of people who read the papers, yet it hasn't been able to dent our paper's circulation in all these years. The decline is because of the lazy and uninspired reporters we have hired lately. They must be found and sacked. *Punto*!'

Knowing his father and his temper, Stefano does not push

his point any further. As soon as they have finished eating, Stefano heads back to his cabin, thinking about what his father said. Somehow, he finds it difficult to agree with Marco.

On the other side of town, Elisabetta is on the phone with her niece Rosa, who is the same age as Stella.

'Zia Elisabetta, you never fail to disappoint me. Never!' says Rosa after hearing about the incidents of the previous night and that morning.

'But, Rosa ...'

'Don't interrupt me, Zia. Your daughter is thirty years old now. In all these years, have you made even the slightest effort to understand what she wants from her life? Even one teeny-weeny bit?'

'She's my only daughter. I know her. I know what she likes and dislikes. What is there—'

'What is there to understand, right? Why should you try to understand her? After all, she is the daughter. It is she who should understand your dreams and continue to fulfil them like she's been doing for all these years. Even if it means crushing her own dreams in the process.'

'I don't understand. What have I done to crush Stella's dreams? I only want her to be happy.'

'Zia, this is Stella's wedding, one of the biggest days of her life, but you took over without even speaking to her once. First, you deprived her of the opportunity to break the news to her family, aunts and cousins. Then, instead of the small, intimate wedding she has always wanted, you announced that there would be a big family wedding in Bergamo.'

'But these are my relatives too, and it will be a big day for me too. Don't I get to have a say?'

'Of course you do. But only after discussing it with Stella, after finding out what Stella wants for her wedding. If you had just spoken to her once, she would have told you why she wants a small wedding instead of the big wedding in Bergamo with hundreds of people, the kind you and your sisters had.

'Zia, times have changed and children these days don't blindly accept whatever their parents say, the way you did when you were young. They know their own minds and want to live their lives their way. We see it every day, even at work. Let me give you an example. Earlier, when Dad ran the bakery by himself, he sold only cakes and cookies. But over time we realised that people no longer want to eat overly rich, cream-laden cakes. They prefer savoury snacks now, and that's what we sell more of in the bakery these days. Could our business have survived if Dad and I had not understood the needs of our customers and had, instead, kept selling cakes only because it was something we had been successfully doing for years?'

'How does that apply to my problem with Stella? Oh, Rosa, what should I do now?' Elisabetta is distraught.

'Zia, if you want to continue having a good relationship with your daughter, you need to start listening to her, just as we listened to our customers because we wanted them to stay with us. Listening is a universal and transferable skill that applies to the family as well as the business. Now you stay put and let me handle things from here. Don't call or message Stella. That'll irritate her even more. Let me plan a weekend outing with her, and you can join us too. Together, we'll listen to her and get her to thaw a little. Bye for now!' Rosa disconnects the call, leaving Elisabetta none the wiser but just a little hopeful.

At the *PdV* office, Stefano is walking across to the circulation department to get the addresses of a few loyal subscribers. He is told that they don't maintain a database of their subscribers' addresses, since they only deliver to the distributors, who deliver onward to the subscribers. Stefano finds this strange but contents himself by taking down the addresses of a few of their biggest distributors.

In the evening, on the way to the cafeteria, Stefano bumps into Roberto, who works in the CFO's office. They went to college together and Stefano also dated his sister for a while. On a whim, Stefano asks Roberto if he would like to accompany him on visits to some distributors the following week. At first, Roberto just laughs. He is an accountant, so his place is behind a desk and not in the field. He isn't keen on wasting his time on silly things that the sales guys—who, in his opinion, chose that profession only because they did badly in college—were meant to do. However, Stefano persists and Roberto reluctantly agrees.

All through the next week, the two boys step out of the office for a couple of hours. Their strategy is to first meet a distributor, collect the names and addresses of a few loyal customers in the neighbourhood and then drop by at their homes for a chat. Most customers are welcoming; some even offer them drinks and snacks. Stefano's experience as a journalist comes in handy in getting the customers to respond to a list of questions he has prepared. He always starts the conversation with something trivial like a comment on the weather or an object in the house. After a few minutes, once the customer has dropped their guard and the conversation has become free-flowing, Stefano starts asking questions about the number of people who live in the house, the medium they prefer for their news—a traditional newspaper, a TV channel or a computer/phone news app—and what they like and dislike about each medium.

After a couple of days, Roberto starts to enjoy the process too. This is very different from what he does inside the office, which mostly involves balancing ledgers and creating profit and loss statements. He comes up with his own list of questions to understand the problems faced by dealers in their transactions with *PdV*. After all, the dealers are also the company's customers, he reasons.

Going by the look on their faces, the dealers are completely shocked by this approach. No one from the business, other than the circulation folks, has ever made the effort to meet them. So far, all their interactions with *PdV* have revolved around sales targets or payment glitches. Being asked for their opinions on what they like or dislike about dealing with *PdV*, what they would like changed, is a first.

Curiosity gets the better of Roberto's boss, the head of the accounts department, and he decides to accompany the boys one afternoon. He enjoys the friendly chats but it is the wealth of information that they are gathering about the news publishing industry, and specifically their own business, that excites him the most. Word gets around amongst senior management and soon other department heads also start wanting to go out to gather information specific to their departments. Marco is aware of the experiment but keeps quiet, allowing his son a free hand.

Over the next few months, everyone who matters in the company, except Marco, gets into the practice of regularly consulting *PdV*'s customers. Stefano feels it is time now to formalise the process and add a certain dose of objectivity and regularity to the activity instead of leaving it to individual whims and fancies. He also realises that it is time he took the idea to his father.

At the next senior management meeting called by Marco, Stefano presents his plan for capturing the voice of the customer. He talks his father and the senior team through the concept of net promoter score, or NPS, as it is popularly known, and explains the process of getting feedback from customers at various touchpoints in their transactions with *PdV*. He explains that to standardise the process, customers' feedback will be taken on a five-point scale, just as the cab company Uber does for its drivers. The concerned team will also have the option of checking back with the customers who have given a very low or very high rating to find out the reason behind the ratings. This data, if tracked regularly, will give the management a handle on things they need to stop doing and what they need to do more of.

When Stefano finishes the presentation, he turns to his father. Over the last few months, Marco has received feedback from several members of the senior management who are now convinced that capturing the voice of the customer is the right way forward for *PdV*. He is proud of Stefano for the hard work he has put in and the brilliant plan he has come up with to fix the problems that *PdV* is facing. He happily gives Stefano the go-ahead to proceed with his plan.

Stefano engages a consulting firm to assist him in setting up the process. Now, the management team's Monday morning meeting starts with a presentation of the previous week's NPS scores from across multiple customer touchpoints and verbatim quotes from customers who have rated their *PdV* experience very high or very low. The conversations in the room have moved from conjecture and speculation to 'Hey, let's change …'

At the Rossi residence, three cars are being loaded for a weekend trip to St. Moritz. Rosa has been able to convince Stella to go with her parents, although it is clear that she is still upset with them. On Friday afternoon, Marco, Elisabetta, Stella, Luca, Stefano, Rosa and her husband drive up to St. Moritz, where Marco's office has booked four suites for two nights at one of the oldest and most luxurious resorts in town. Throughout the car ride and later at the hotel, Stella remains aloof and doesn't talk to either Elisabetta or Marco. Her responses to their questions are limited to monosyllables or nods without eye contact. Elisabetta is filled with anger and sadness towards her daughter.

On Saturday evening, Rosa asks Stella and Elisabetta to take a walk with her around the estate. Rosa realises that it is time to attempt a reconciliation between mother and daughter. On the other side of the resort, another family has gathered for a wedding. From a distance, the wedding arrangements look classy and elegant, the entire area done up in accents of muted pink and gold. From the pavilion to the flowers and the band, and the guests in their best designer attire, it makes for a very happy picture.

While Stella is admiring the scene, Rosa asks her a few provocative questions that seem to suggest that this is the kind of wedding that Elisabetta wants to organise for Stella but Stella isn't letting her do it. The sight of the wedding and the tone in which Rosa asks the questions overwhelm Stella, and she finally breaks down. Between sobs, she says that any girl would want a wedding like this or even better. But her mother's decision to announce the wedding on her own to the rest of the family and telling them the kind of wedding Stella was going to have without speaking to her even once made her feel like a child. She complains that all her life her parents encouraged her to become independent and gave her the space to decide for herself, a power she has never misused. Then why now, at the most crucial juncture of her life, were they treating her like a child and taking away her agency?

As Stella sobs out her story, Elisabetta realises her mistake. In her enthusiasm over the wedding, she failed to consider that Stella has the right to decide what her dream day should look like. She wishes now that on the night the couple had come home to tell them about their decision, she had asked them about what they wanted to do before announcing the wedding plans to the rest of the family. That way she could have tweaked her plans as per Stella's wishes and would not have made her feel like a child.

Elisabetta steps forward, hugs Stella and apologises. She tells her how much she loves her and how her excitement for the wedding got the better of her. She promises Stella that Marco and she will sit down with her and her fiancé the next weekend and understand from the couple the kind of wedding they want, where they want it to be held and who they want to invite. From this simple act of listening and with this promise made, peace is restored in the Rossi family.

Meanwhile, Stefano is getting to understand the business better. More importantly, since he has a first-hand understanding of the customers, his word has started to carry weight. He has begun to draw respect for his own knowledge and hard work, not just because he is Marco's son.

At one of the Monday meetings, Stefano asks Marco if he and the other department heads could set aside some time, a fortnight later, for him to take them through a strategy presentation for the business. Marco agrees, as does every department head. This will be the first time that the department heads get a say in deciding the strategy for *PdV*. Usually, whatever Marco decides is followed by everyone in the company.

At the strategy meeting, Stefano puts forward a vision for the firm, based on the knowledge he has gathered from speaking to their existing and old customers. Since every department head has been interacting with customers too, there is a coherence between what Stefano is saying and what they have observed during their customer visits.

After this, Stefano spends the next two weeks having one-on-one meetings with the department heads, discussing their future plans and the investments required to execute them. This leads to the creation of a strategic business plan for the firm, with each of the department heads making individual presentations after Stefano has laid out the broad path they will navigate over the next five years.

Marco, who always has the last word in any meeting, sits through numerous long meetings listening to his team and their plans for *PdV*. The proposals are backed by hard deliverables, stated as short-term milestones and long-term goals. They are so convincing that Marco has no choice but to give his assent and sign off on the plans.

That night, the Rossi family—Marco, Elisabetta, Stella, Stefano and the new entrant Luca—raises a toast with a vintage wine that Marco has been saving in his cellar for over a decade.

Marco and Elisabetta exchange a glance that suggests they have come to a mutual understanding. Their children are all grown up and it's time they started listening to them and including their voices in both family and business decisions.

They are glad it isn't too late to adapt.

Here are some statements that you should respond to for the business that you are a part of, as an owner or a manager. Remember to respond honestly.

The statements must be answered in a yes/no format. If there are any statements that are not relevant to your business, put a cross against them.

- ☐ We have at least five ways of accessing the voice of our customers (listening into calls, customer home visits, etc.) that are available to people across all functions and levels.
- ☐ For the CEO+2 levels, we track how often individuals have had one-on-one interactions with customers.
- ☐ Whenever individuals from the CEO+2 levels interact with customers, they circulate their observations to the group.
- ☐ Feedback from customer-facing individuals to non-customer-facing colleagues is articulated in a relatable manner and comprehensible language.
- ☐ Net promoter score (NPS) is measured for every

customer touchpoint and is a key performance indicator for all employees.

- ☐ The top five reasons for customers who have provided low NPS ratings are compiled, presented to and discussed by the CEO+2 levels, once a month.
- ☐ Actions agreed to during this meeting are recorded and outstanding actions pertaining to previous meetings are reviewed.
- ☐ The last time our NPS score dipped for three consecutive weeks, we commenced recovery within thirty days.
- ☐ Every process change that could impact customer experience is first tested with a few customers and implemented only after it succeeds with them.
- ☐ Every individual in the CEO+2 levels has worked in a customer-facing role once during their career.

Now consider the statements to which you have responded with a 'No'. Discuss and reflect on these within your company, read more about the **voice of the customer** and/or ask some experts about how to apply these statements to your specific case.

Doing this could help you steer your business in the direction of your customers and not away from them.

3

STICKY PRODUCTS AND REPEAT CUSTOMERS

Crafting compelling propositions

Geeta asks James to pass her some banana fritters as she digs into an ackee and saltfish breakfast that has become her staple food every morning. Her mind goes back to the last five years that the two of them have been living and working in Jamaica.

James grew up in the quiet beach town of Brighton in the UK and went to the University of Bath for his MBA. That's where he met Geeta, who had come to the UK from Assam, a hilly state in the eastern region of India. After graduation, they both found jobs in London and moved in together.

For ten years, Geeta worked at a telecom firm as an analyst. Her job involved identifying cohorts of customers displaying similar behaviour patterns. The analysis helped the commercial team retain the customers who were showing signs of unsubscribing by offering them discounts or moving them to less expensive packages. It also helped the sales team identify customers who were ready to buy higher-end products and subscribe to more services. This practice of upselling played a huge role in increasing the firm's revenue.

In the same ten years, James changed his job twice. He first worked at a personal products and cosmetics company and later at a packaged foods firm. During his tenure there, he added many more variants, colours and flavours to the product lines, which helped in revenue growth for both firms.

The common thread in their work is the desire to provide products that cater to the needs of low-paying customers, leading to revenue growth for their companies and generation of profits for the investors. Over the years, James and Geeta have often, at the dinner table, thrashed out issues they face at work, strongly believing that such discussions help in keeping their relationship exciting.

Being avid fans of cricket and admirers of Chris Gayle from the West Indies, five years ago, they decided to go to Jamaica for a vacation, more as a pilgrimage to Gayle's hometown. However, fate had much more in store for them.

While in Jamaica, they accidently met Coomar, a third-generation Indian migrant whose grandfather had come over as a farm labourer. Coomar's father had bought land in Jamaica and started cultivation of sugarcane. When Coomar took over from his father, he had switched the crop type from sugarcane to bamboo, which he thought was easier to grow.

Over the years, he had purchased the neighbouring fields, becoming Jamaica's largest bamboo farmer. At his plant, bamboo was converted into pulp to be sold to paper mills to make newsprint.

The evening before James and Geeta were supposed to fly back to London, they visited Coomar's house. Over drinks, the conversation became serious and turned to Coomar's business.

'Coomar, you are sitting on a gold mine with your acres and acres of bamboo trees but you are just wasting it all away by restricting your activities to only selling pulp,' Geeta had exclaimed.

'Geeta, growing things is all I know. That's what my father did and that's what I do best. We are farmers, not manufacturers.'

'But what you don't realise is that it's the manufacturers who are cornering the big bucks out of what could be your value chain while all you're getting is some loose change. Coomar, do you even realise how much money the guys who buy bamboo pulp from you are making by converting it into paper, medicines, kitchenware and what not? Do you have any idea?'

'That's because, like jewellers who know how to take a piece of metal and convert it into beautiful jewellery, the people I sell my bamboo pulp to know how to manufacture it into something useful. They deserve the money they make.'

'But even you can do that, Coomar!' said Geeta in protest.

'Guys, I know what I know. B2B is my strength. I sell to

converters who understand the B2C space. For me, that's a black hole and I don't want to lose my shirt doing what I don't understand.'

'You can always hire people who know the B2C game and make them do the work. I mean, James and I work for firms because we understand the B2C game. We help them in transforming their raw materials into finished products that they can sell directly to the consumers.'

'Hmm ... So, are you guys willing to put your money where your mouth is?' questioned Coomar.

'What do you mean? We don't have any money to put into your business.'

'I'm not asking you for money. Your money is your time and expertise. Are you willing to leave your jobs in London, shift to Jamaica and help me build a B2C organisation and business?'

'Are you kidding? We don't understand the bamboo business.'

'You did not understand the telecom, food or cosmetics business either when you started working in such companies. But now you do. That's because you understand business and value creation. Come, join me as partners and let's build value together.'

'You can't afford our salaries,' joked Geeta.

'No, I can't. But I can offer you a 20 per cent stake in the business for the time you spend working for me. If over the next ten years, together we end up building the kind of business you both have been talking about for the last week,

I'll transfer 20 per cent of the business in your names at the end of the ten years. Deal?'

Three months later, James and Geeta relocated to Jamaica. Night after night, they sat with Coomar, brainstorming on a list of products and ready-to-use options that could be manufactured from bamboo and taken to the market, apart from the pulp that Coomar was already selling to paper mills.

One evening, the discussion went something like this.

'Instead of supplying pulp to paper mills who convert it to newsprint, why don't we set up a small paper-making unit ourselves and make toilet paper, kitchen rolls, coffee filters, paper cups, etc.?' suggested James.

'This sounds like a good space to start and could come under the paper products division,' agreed Geeta.

'I've also read somewhere that bamboo shoots are a good source of proteins, amino acids, carbs, minerals and vitamins. Different parts of bamboo have different medicinal properties and can be used to treat stomach disorders, reduce body sugar, act as antioxidants and help in controlling inflammation. Black bamboo is used for treating coughs and mucus, lung inflammation, strokes, fever and headaches,' added James.

'So does that mean there is room for a natural medicines division as well?' asked Coomar.

'Looks like there is,' replied James.

'Do you know that bamboo can be moulded into kitchenware such as forks, spoons, cutting boards, bowls, etc.?

And converted to board, bamboo is a great substitute for ply and can be used to make flooring, screens and veneers, and furniture like chairs, beds, racks, lamp shades, roller blinds, etc.,' said Geeta.

'Wow! So, we can set up a kitchenware, furniture and building materials division too,' James said excitedly.

'What about a fabrics division?' said Geeta, joining in the excitement. 'I read somewhere that bamboo converted to yarn creates an airy, permeable, soft fabric that is ideal for bedding, innerwear, towels, diapers, etc.'

'Guys, aren't we biting off more than we can chew? Let us attack things one at a time and do a good job of whatever we do,' said the ever-cautious Coomar.

'Just because we've thought about it doesn't mean we plan to invest in it tonight. Let us make a list of all that can be done. After that we'll prioritise and attack them one business at a time,' suggested Geeta to Coomar.

Coomar was still apprehensive but decided not to say anything more. On the other hand, James and Geeta kept throwing ideas at each other late into the night, ignoring Coomar.

They decided to sell their products under the brand name 'Bamboo Dance', which clearly conveyed that the products were made from bamboo apart from sounding vibrant, youthful and lively enough to connect well with the new generation.

Geeta and James chose their roles in the new business based on their previous work experiences. Geeta chose to head the commercial function while James took upon himself the responsibility of product management. His job involved identifying suitable products for each division and creating a go-to market strategy for them. On the other hand, Geeta decided the pricing for the products and managed the factories, making sure that every product they sold was delivering a margin that provided an adequate return on the capital that Coomar had invested.

Five years have passed since then. It has been a roller-coaster ride with ups, downs, some slow rises and many rapid falls. However, there has never been a dull moment.

In fact, in the first year itself, they managed to launch three of the five divisions they had identified. They started by setting up a paper mill to manufacture various paper products, which they initially supplied only to local standalone stores and store chains. The brown face tissues, kitchen and toilet rolls, which looked and felt different from the white paper products that the customers had been using for decades, were an instant hit. The company had a tough time coping with the demand until they increased their production capacity. A year later, they set up an exports division, appointed agents in a handful of neighbouring countries and started selling the paper products in six countries, including the US and parts of South America.

Initially, the response from markets outside of Jamaica wasn't so great. To find out the reason for this, Geeta visited a couple of towns in Cuba and the US. What she realised was that the Bamboo Dance tissues were priced at almost two times the price of regular paper tissues that were being sold in shops there. Tissues being voluminous products, the cost of transportation of finished goods from Jamaica to these countries was high. Geeta decided that they would find local manufacturers in each of these markets to whom they would ship the pulp from Jamaica. She figured this would lead to a reduction of transportation costs, and their product would be able to match the price of the local products. Once the company managed to set up local manufacturing in every country they sold in, the sales of the product took off. Sales and margins grew everywhere.

Unfortunately, the success of the paper tissues could not be replicated for the other products produced by this division, like cups and coffee filters. These products were showing no movement off the store shelves whatsoever, and retailers were returning large quantities of unsold stocks. These returned stocks had to be destroyed, leading to an overall operating loss for the firm in the first two years, despite the superb sales of tissues and napkins. Geeta decided to undertake some consumer research to get to the root of the problem. From local stores, she found out the contact details of a handful of customers who had bought these products. She also asked the stores to give her details of some of their regular customers who had not bought Bamboo Dance cups or filters and had instead chosen to buy the same products of a different brand. She followed this up by contracting with a market research agency to question both these sets of customers.

The market research agency found that non-buyers outnumbered buyers by a mile. The buyers were the elite of Jamaica, people who wanted to buy exclusively eco-friendly products, regardless of how expensive they were. The non-buyers had found the price of Bamboo Dance to be much higher than that of regular paper cups and filters that were not made with bamboo pulp. The lesson was clear. Mass market customers were willing to switch to eco-friendly products only if they were priced the same as the products that they were already using. But if they came at a higher cost, then it didn't matter to them whether the product they were using was made from an eco-friendly material or not.

Unlike in the case of the tissue papers, where the company had managed to reduce their price by changing the manufacturing process, in the case of paper cups and filters, it was difficult to do the same. They found that making paper cups from bamboo pulp at a price lower than that of the cups made from the usual material was just not possible. Also, the volumes were too small for the manufacturing to be subcontracted as in the case of paper tissues. Hence, they had no choice but to discontinue this product line.

Coomar expressed his displeasure to James and Geeta. That's why he had stuck to only supplying the pulp and had not gone into manufacturing, he said. He had always felt that selling to stores was a risky proposition. What hurt James and Geeta the most was when he said, 'I thought you guys knew how to test a product's reception in the market before betting the house on it. Seems I was mistaken.'

Geeta and James discussed what Coomar had said over dinner that night.

'What Coomar said today made me feel horrible,' said Geeta.

'Yeah. Me too. Wish we'd discovered this before getting into commercial production of cups and filters.'

'I wonder how we missed it. We never did in our ten years of working for other companies.'

'We didn't because as employees of large companies, we had specialists whose job was to test every product with live customers before clearing it for commercial production. They would come back to us with what the customers had said about the product, where they'd liked it or not, how often they were willing to buy it and what price they were willing to pay for it. Based on all that information, we would make modifications in the product or its manufacturing process or its price and launch it in the market. If we felt that the modifications were not possible, we would go back to the drawing board or consign the product to the bin,' explained James.

'I guess, as entrepreneurs, it's now our job to find out all this information before launching a product.'

'I think we were also blinded by the success of tissue paper and felt we could replicate it for other products as well. Never mind, lesson learnt. Never again will we make the same mistake,' reassured James.

Around three years ago, James and Geeta kicked off two other divisions—kitchenware and fabrics—albeit in a small way.

Two small production units were set up to manufacture a limited range of products, and the company started off by making their products available only in a couple of large stores in Jamaica.

James and Geeta had just returned from a three-day cross-functional strategy meet at Bridgetown, Barbados. The sales guys were gung-ho about the products from the kitchenware and fabrics range because they were managing to sell most of the limited quantity of products that were being produced. Geeta, however, pointed out that demand for products from these two divisions was only coming from new stores that agreed to stock the products but not from stores where they had already introduced the products. Sales in such stores were either stagnant or declining.

To this, the sales team said that demand generation was not their job. Their responsibility was to find new stores that would stock the products and to replenish shelves of existing stores with fresh stocks once they got sold. They were not responsible for making sure that the demand from the stores remained constant. Geeta found this attitude disconcerting but kept quiet, deciding she would discuss this with James later.

Later over drinks, Geeta casually asked some of the sales guys what they thought was the reason that they were not getting repeat orders for Bamboo Dance's kitchenware and fabric products. They told her that even though the kitchenware products produced by Bamboo Dance were lighter and their finish superior to that of traditional wooden products, the product range was very limited compared to other more traditional brands. 'A kitchen can't have ten utensils that all look different from each other,' they said. The fabric sales teams gave Geeta similar feedback. They also informed Geeta that to counter the Bamboo Dance tissue paper, other tissue brands started paying stores for every piece that they displayed on their shelves. Because of this, the number of Bamboo Dance products that were stocked in store shelves was very low. The relatively lower visibility for Bamboo Dance's products, according to them, was impacting customer demand.

Today they are sitting in their home over a breakfast of ackee and saltfish and discussing everything they learnt at the strategy meet.

'If Bamboo Dance tissue papers, which were selling so well, are having trouble creating repeat demand and if our kitchenware and fabrics are not being bought by those customers who regularly use and like our tissue paper, what hope can we have for the products of the other two divisions that are still in the pipeline?' asks Geeta, looking worried.

'That's what I've been thinking about too. And if paper is all that this brand ends up selling, then why do we need this big organisation that we have created? Coomar could have just stuck to producing pulp, or at best diversified into making paper. We were the ones who convinced him to think beyond pulp and paper.'

'You're beginning to sound like the pessimist that you are.

Relax, the world is not coming to an end anytime soon. We've always managed to find solutions to our problems in the past and we will do so this time as well.'

This is not the first time that James and Geeta are having this conversation. Creating and maintaining consumer demand has always been at the top of their minds, even when they lived and worked in London. They have had long discussions on why TV and telecom service companies refer to their customers as subscribers. Is it because once such companies get a customer to subscribe, the customer is likely to stick to the same brand for years on end, paying the billed charges on the due date, month after month? And how do such companies ensure the satisfaction of their customers over a long period of time?

From her experience at a telecom firm, Geeta is aware that to maintain the loyalty of their customers, such companies constantly innovate and introduce exciting new services, new price plans, upgrades and other offers. Together, James and Geeta have often wondered why such models are not used by consumer goods companies too; after all, customers buy soaps, detergents, cookies, chips, etc., as frequently as they watch TV or make phone calls. Why can't consumer goods companies have subscribers too? Subscribers who will buy the same brand month after month or who will take an annual subscription to get a particular quantity of goods delivered to them every week or month, irrespective of whether the previous quantities of such goods have finished or not? Also, why is it that consumer goods companies can never bank upon regular customers—customers who used a product once, are satisfied with it and keep buying it again and again, without looking at any of the other brands available in the market? Why does the company have to keep advertising the product just to keep it fresh in the customer's mind? Similarly, why won't a satisfied customer of a product willingly buy another product of the same brand, knowing that the new product will be of the same quality as the one they are satisfied with? After all, telecom and TV subscribers choose to stick to the same brand while subscribing to additional services even if other brands are providing additional services at a lower cost. Is it because the cost of changing brands again and again is very high, or is it inertia? Or is it that people who sell physical products such as consumer goods have never tried to look at their customers as subscribers? And if so, what can such companies do to convert their customers into subscribers?

Geeta is reminded of this conversation now, as she and James are brainstorming ideas on how to increase and create demand for Bamboo Dance products. She also recalls seeing a subscription offer a week ago of a 10 per cent discount for her soap on an e-commerce site.

'How about we print "Reorder Now" somewhere towards the end of the tissue roll? This way the customer will not only be reminded to buy another roll while some of it is still left but since our details will be printed next to "Reorder Now", they will also be reminded to buy from us instead of a competitor brand. We could also add a phone number there where customers can text their residential post code. We can then coordinate direct delivery to the customer's residence from the nearest store that stocks our products. We can also have a Bamboo Dance app that can help customers place an order by just pressing a button,' says James.

'Great idea. Did you think of it in the loo this morning? Sorry, I forgot to replace the roll after it finished last night,' says Geeta mischievously.

'Haha! You can get a fantastic idea anywhere. Listen, if a small portion of customers, say 10–15 per cent, reorder because of our message on the tissue rolls, it would be a great boost to sales. How about also offering a 10 per cent discount to customers who commit to a year's supplies? Every time their roll finishes, they can just click a button on our app, and we'll ship a packet to them. The cost incurred to give such discounts will be much less than what we spend on advertisements to remind our customers to buy our product.'

'Fantastic! However, let's not get carried away. Let's try to implement these ideas manually first, putting to work our large sales and distribution teams. If it's a success, then we can invest in processes and equipment to automate receiving of orders and delivery of products.'

'Agreed,' says James with a big smile on his face.

In the next set of Bamboo Dance tissue rolls that are manufactured, the 'Reorder Now' message is inserted. Twenty per cent of the customers who purchase the message-printed rolls text back asking for a reorder. This response rate is higher than any that James has ever seen before, and he is confident that this will take care of the issue of repeat demand that the sales teams raised. What makes James even more happy is knowing that the increase in demand for tissue rolls has taken place without them having to buy more shelf space or paying for signages in stores. From there on, the words 'Reorder Now' become a feature of every roll they manufacture and sell.

The annual subscription model doesn't find the same success. Since there are such few takers for it, the company decides to abandon the model in its entirety. That evening James and Geeta chat about it.

'I am guessing that people have commitment phobia when it comes to toilet rolls. That's why they rejected the annual subscription model even while accepting the reorder option.'

'Haha! Well put, James.'

'We are lucky that of the couple of good ideas we had, at least one worked for us, while the other we were able to discard without having wasted too much of our money. Yet, I'm wondering, is this really our job? Why aren't the product teams coming up with these ideas instead?'

'Could it be because the ideas we came up with were not to do with product creation but customer retention?'

'How does that matter? Should a product manager just go off to sleep after a product has been created? Is keeping the customer interested in the product not a part of their job profile too?'

'What I actually meant was that while product creation requires intuitive and creative skills, retaining a customer requires gathering data from customers, crunching it to make sense and then devising ways to make customers buy again and again by using the data obtained,' says Geeta.

'What I'm hearing you say is that we need two different profiles of people to do these jobs because it is difficult to find both these sets of skills in just one person. Would it make sense, therefore, to split the existing products team into two teams, one that takes charge of creating new products and the other that devises ways to retain customers? We could call them by some other name.'

'I think it does. We could call them the customer acquisition and the customer retention teams.'

'While we are at it, let's add a third team to the group and call it the revenue enhancement team. These guys will create premium versions of the same product that would have higher margins and find ways to get existing customers to upgrade to these products. They can also come up with ideas to sell our other products to existing customers who are still hesitant to try them.'

'Great idea! We may need to hire a few more people for each of these teams with the right set of skills and experience, but I'm confident that in the long run, this extra expense will pay off with higher sales,' says James.

Later, when the product team is informed about the team being split into three smaller divisions with truncated yet specialised roles for each division, most members of the team feel that the dilution of their responsibilities demonstrates a lack of confidence in their abilities by the management. They are not happy with this split.

While Geeta is worried about the impact of this change on team morale, James justifies it by saying, 'Humans resist change yet adapt to it quickly. Don't worry, this too shall sink in soon.'

Geeta now starts focusing on the kitchenware and fabrics divisions. She decides to walk around in the stores that stock Bamboo Dance kitchenware and fabrics. She also watches what their competitors—the traditional and old-school sellers of these products—are selling. She finds that Bamboo Dance's range of kitchenware does not cover even a third of all kitchenware options that are available in these stores, whereas their competitors have vast ranges of kitchenware products. Her observation aligns with what the sales guys complained about at the strategy meet.

Next, she walks into James's office and engages in a conversation with the products teams from the two divisions. James is in the office too. Surprised to see Geeta there, he joins the group but watches the interaction silently.

Geeta starts by gently probing the team about why they chose certain kitchenware products to be manufactured by Bamboo Dance and not the other products belonging to the same range. For example, what made them pick spoons and forks and not ladles?

They tell her that right from the start, the team decided to be sensible and chose only those products to manufacture from each category that promised high volumes. They decided not to experiment with niche products. In addition, they decided that they would go for only one variant of each product instead of producing the same product in multiple styles and colours. Geeta realises that while all these appeared to be pragmatic calls from a sales perspective, it means that customers can't have all the utensils and cutlery in their kitchens made from bamboo. Because of Bamboo Dance's limited range, customers are being forced to own a mismatched set of utensils and cutlery, some made from bamboo, some from wood and some from metal. Moreover, even if they do decide to buy Bamboo Dance's kitchenware, there is no variety to choose from, since there is only one style of spoons or forks that Bamboo Dance manufactures. She can finally understand why their kitchenware range is not selling at all.

The team informs her that it was James who asked them to keep the range and variety of the products limited, since he did not want to repeat the experience of dumping large quantities of products that didn't sell, like they had had to with the paper cups and filters. His exact words were: 'Just make sure that you produce what will sail with the customer. Don't try to float paper boats.'

Geeta probes further and asks the team whether they have ever had a conversation with their colleagues from the paper production team to discuss possible synergies between divisions, since the latter is doing very well and has customers in many countries. To that, she is told that paper production is completely different from kitchenware and fabrics, and the only thing that is common is that all the products are made from bamboo. The team felt that because of these differences, something that worked for the paper division may not work for them. Then she asks them that, if not their own colleagues, did the team at least study their competitors' products to find out what was working for customers and what was not. To this, the team tells her that they refrained from doing so because they didn't want to hinder innovation.

By now Geeta is quietly seething at the complacency of the team, and while leaving she says to them in a sarcastic tone, 'You are not Henry Ford, and this is not 1908 that people will buy whatever you produce, even if all you produce is one model, one variant. Wake up and smell the coffee. Customers have been spoilt over the years. They already have more choices than they need, yet they keep looking for more. If you don't pull up your straps and start providing more choices, your brand will not be the consumers' choice.'

On reaching home that evening, Geeta quickly realises that James is upset with her. She confronts him over dinner and asks him what's wrong.

'Who gave you the right to walk into my office and start interrogating my team members?' asks James angrily.

'I was only trying to check on some of the things I had noticed in the stores I visited yesterday,' replies Geeta.

'Whatever questions you had, you could've asked me, like you've always done, instead of terrorising the youngsters. We are together every evening and morning, and you can talk to me anytime.'

'James, I was only trying to help.'

'Help? It sounded more like an audit to me.'

'Not at all. That wasn't my intention at all. I'm sorry if it appeared like that.'

'Geeta, your questions felt very hostile today. My team and I are trying our best to make the kitchenware and fabrics divisions a success. But increasingly, I have started feeling tired of all this. This entrepreneurship idea sounded very romantic five years ago but that was because we were full of enthusiasm and were looking at the situation from the outside. The lack of intelligent and specialised people to bounce ideas with and listening to Coomar's repeated taunts about profitability and profligacy were bad enough. But now even you have started auditing my work and spying on what I do. I have had enough.'

'I think you are overreacting, James. Things are not as bad as you are making them out to be.'

'Geeta, there are days when I regret chucking my London job and coming here where resources are limited but the need to prove myself in spite of the odds is much higher.'

'My dear James, don't think this way. I'm sorry I wasn't more sensitive towards the work difficulties you are facing. It was never my intention to walk into your workplace unannounced and spy on you. In the future, I will always come to you first.'

'It's okay, Geeta.'

'Now, cheer up. Why don't we drive out to Negril tomorrow and stay over the night? Just to relax and chill,' suggests Geeta.

James and Geeta are both fond of long drives and, even though Jamaica is a small island, there are several drives that are breathtaking, and most of them culminate on a sandy white beach.

Next morning, on the way to Negril, Geeta tries to broach the topic of the last evening with James. This time she is determined to convey her viewpoint to James in a sensitive manner.

'James, have I ever told you the story of how I learnt to cook? It was such a long time ago, while I was still in India. I have come a long way since then, especially when it comes to desserts.'

'You are an expert at desserts, Geeta. I love eating the sweet things you make,' says James with a smile.

'Thanks, James. But do you know when I started out with cooking, I never thought of becoming a dessert specialist? My mother was the cook in our family, but she would make me help her by asking me to do the chopping, frying, etc.'

'Okay. So how did you progress from the basics of cooking?'

'The first dish I tried was a pork curry that my mother made very well. It came out so bad that even the street dog refused it.'

'That must've been so embarrassing. Did you stop cooking after that and go back to cleaning and chopping only?'

'No, I didn't. I kept trying my hand at various dishes and eventually realised that I wasn't very good with meat but I could do a decent enough job with vegetables.'

'So, did the cooking of vegetables for every meal become your responsibility after that?'

'Not really. I only cooked veggies when my mom wasn't well. On other days, I refrained from cooking because I didn't want everyone to compare my cooking with hers.'

'But then how come you shifted to desserts? Was your mother good at those too?' asked James.

'My mother hardly had the time to make any desserts after cooking three meals for the entire family. Sometimes Dad would bring home payas or kheer, milk- and rice-based desserts, from the market. I used to love having them. That's when I thought instead of trying to cook the same things that my mother already cooked well, why don't I try something different. That's when I tried my hand at desserts.'

'So, did the first dessert you made come out perfect?'

'No, it was a disaster. The rice pudding was lumpy, and the milk had a burnt flavour. However, my brother was very sweet. He ate it all and weakly commented that it would have been even better had the pudding been cooked for less time.'

'So, did you perfect the rice pudding the next time you made it?' asks James.

'No. I thought what's the point of making desserts that Dad could easily get for us from the market. I switched to baking instead. The first couple of things I baked, I made small portions only for myself. Only after I was satisfied that the dish tasted right did I bake it for the entire family.'

'That was sensible.'

'As I got better at it, I started baking with confidence and tried my hand at many new things.'

'What was your mom's reaction to your baking?'

'She was always supportive and would often suggest a few tweaks that would help improve the dish. My brother encouraged me a lot too. Every time I baked a dessert, he would go out of his way and drop me to my college the next day on his bike. That was a good incentive to bake more and more.'

'Now I know that the excellent desserts I get to have are the result of a lot of hard work on your part and encouragement from your family.'

'That's true. But sometimes I wonder that had I not tried my hand at cooking meals and failed miserably, I would have never switched to desserts. If I had been mediocre at it, I may have stuck to it and never have found my expertise in cooking.'

'That's one way to look at it,' says James.

'Well, don't you think the work we do is a bit like that too? I mean we have to try our hand at a few things first. If they don't work, then we have to move to the next thing and keep moving until we find our expertise. Just because one thing doesn't work, it doesn't mean we give up on the whole idea. After all, I didn't give up on the whole idea of cooking, did I?'

'Hmm … you are right.'

'Another thing that is similar between my initial cooking attempts and our efforts at creating new products that succeed at Bamboo Dance is that both things need experimentation and encouragement. Just like I experimented with different types of dessert, we have to allow our employees to experiment. We can't get angry with them if they fail initially. On the contrary, we need to encourage people to experiment and fail because failure makes people discover new things,' continued Geeta.

'Hmm,' ponders James aloud. 'I'm listening.'

'Experiments carried out in small proportions can help restrict losses, just like I initially tried baking small batches of desserts, until I got it right.'

'Makes sense.'

'And James, don't forget my mother's and brother's roles in my whole cooking journey. My mom wanted me to learn cooking, and my brother wanted to eat new desserts. Hence, together they helped and incentivised baking for me. If all stakeholders have an incentive in the outcome, it makes sure that the outcome is great.'

'You have given me a lot to think about, Geeta. Give me some time to ponder on it.'

'That's fine, James. Take your time.'

For the rest of the journey, both remain silent, watching a mesmerising sunset as they enter Negril.

Later in the evening, James and Geeta are having dinner at their favourite Blue Mahoe Restaurant. While James has his favourite dish, oxtail, Geeta settles for fried chicken.

After remaining silent for a while, James holds out his hand to Geeta and says, 'My dear, as always, you're right. What you said about creating new products is correct. Creating products that customers would like to buy and continue buying is not easy. However, if we're willing to experiment and adapt with every failure, we can end up creating a sustainable range of bamboo products.'

Geeta smiles at James, relieved that James has found his optimistic outlook once again.

Here are some statements that you should respond to for the business that you are a part of, as an owner or a manager. Remember to respond honestly.

The statements must be answered in a yes/no format. If there are any statements that are not relevant to your business, put a cross against them.

- ☐ The pricing, distribution, etc. of our products goes through real-life testing with live customers prior to their widespread launch.
- ☐ In the last year, we have experimented with more products than were eventually launched.
- ☐ We have a competitive product, with multiple variants, for each of our target segments.
- ☐ The people responsible for creating new products are incentivised for the successful adoption of these products.
- ☐ Incentives are proportionate to the profitability of the product.

- ☐ Our product team has different people responsible for acquiring customers, retaining them and increasing revenue from the retained customers.
- ☐ We have conversion targets for every retention and revenue enhancement campaign. The viability of every campaign is tracked, and we have not had a loss-making campaign in the last year.
- ☐ We survey customers who have stopped purchasing our products to identify the reasons for doing so. This is followed by tweaks to products and processes based on the information gathered. The improvements are communicated to customers via advertisements.
- ☐ We track customers who use more than one of our products. We target to increase the proportion of customers using multiple products of our company by 10 per cent every year.
- ☐ Product managers are rotated between categories and no person handles the same category for more than two years.

Now consider the statements to which you have responded with a 'No'. Discuss and reflect on these within your company, read more about **compelling propositions** and/or ask some experts about how to apply these statements to your specific case.

Doing this could prevent your company from missing out on new product opportunities while continuing to grow revenues and profits from the products you already have.

4

IN SEARCH OF THE MOST RELIABLE PRODUCT

Aiming for lower failure, faster recovery

Nur is running late for her flight to Seattle. She disembarks from the cab at Newark Airport and marches towards her boarding gate, almost running. Just as the final call for passengers to board her flight is announced, her phone starts ringing. She picks up the call without breaking her stride. It is her ex-boss, Amir, calling from Malaysia. She is surprised to see his name on the phone screen as they haven't spoken in years.

'Nur, how are you?' asks Amir. 'Why are you sounding out of breath?'

'I'm at Newark Airport running towards my boarding gate to catch a flight to Seattle.'

'Oh I can see you are busy right now. I'll call back later to discuss this in detail, but for now I want you to consider just one thing. As you know, I'm on the local board of Breze. It is one of the biggest air conditioner brands in the world. I want you to join Breze as the CEO for Malaysia.'

Nur is surprised at the offer but tells Amir that she will call him back once she lands in Seattle to discuss this further with him. Saying a quick goodbye, she hangs up.

It is only when she is sitting quietly in her plush business-class seat, sipping on orange juice, that she lets her mind wander to what Amir said. The call has surprised her, though in a pleasant way. Nur worked with Amir for almost fifteen years in Malaysia before moving to the US with one of the largest consumer durables brands in the world. After ten years with that company and various assignments in the sales and strategy departments, she now heads the home appliances category for the US market, and lives in Metuchen, New Jersey.

Amir was a demanding boss, and yet, he was revered by anyone who ever worked with him because of his attention to detail and his ability to think through to the next three moves. Someone once said, 'Amir is the only one playing chess while everyone else is playing ludo.' Amir is known to look after the people he thinks are bright and diligent, even though he never lets them know what he thinks of them. Calls like today's would have gone only to the people on his A list.

Nur and her husband, Adam, who works for a consulting firm, have been contemplating a move back to Malaysia as neither of their parents are getting any younger. Getting them to move to the US is not an option, as every time Nur and Adam have suggested that, their parents have refused to leave their homes, where they have friends and social lives. Neither Nur nor Adam has a sibling, leaving them with no choice but to move back to Malaysia to be close to their parents at a stage when they need their children the most.

Immediately on landing in Seattle, Nur calls Adam and tells him about Amir's call and his offer. They discuss the subject at home for a couple of days as well as with a couple of close friends. The next weekend, Nur gives her consent to join Breze. She doesn't even bother to discuss the compensation package with Amir because she knows that Amir always has her back. Meanwhile, Adam too approaches his boss at the consulting firm to ask for a position in Malaysia.

Three months later, on a Sunday, Amir and Nur land in Kuala Lumpur, with ten large suitcases and a container that is following them by sea. Nur formally joins her office the next day itself. She is welcomed by the members of Breze's board at a special meeting convened to introduce her to them.

Later, after brief introductions with the members of her team, she sits down with them for a brief update on the previous week's performance, something that seems to be a weekly routine. That's when she discovers that Breze's share of new AC sales is at the fourth place in a six-player market, even though they have the largest installed base of air conditioners. This development startles her because till then, she was under the impression that Breze was the market leader. She realises that at this rate, it won't be long before Breze loses its leadership status in the installed base as well. Whatever else is discussed in the meeting room after this shocking revelation does not register with her. She rushes out of to her room as soon as the meeting is over and asks her assistant to connect her with Amir.

When Nur tells Amir about what she has just discovered, Amir sounds his usual 'Captain Cool' self. That's a name those fond of him often use—a nod to his imperturbable demeanour. It seems he is aware of Breze's dwindling market share. When Nur asks him why he didn't tell her about this situation earlier, he asks, 'Would you have agreed to join us if I'd told you all this? Obviously not. However, I'm confident that if there is one person who can turn things around for Breze, it's you. Now get on with the job and let me know if there is any help you need. *Selamat Tinggal.*'

The fact that Amir knew about the situation and didn't warn her worries Nur, but his faith in her abilities also boosts her confidence. She suspects that the reason things are so bad in Breze is because maybe the company has not adapted successfully to the changing competitive landscape of the air-conditioner industry.

Over the next few days, Nur holds several meetings with customers, sellers, employees and partners of Breze to understand how the situation turned so bad. She knows that until and unless she understands the root cause of the problem, she won't be able to fix the situation.

Nur asks her team to name two members from each team responsible for the different functions in the company. She specifically requests for people who are articulate and have been around for some time. She speaks to each nominated person at great length, asking them their opinions about the current condition of Breze and why it has fallen from a position of market dominance to the fourth place in a six-player market.

People are happy to talk openly with Nur, who listens to them without saying much. She discovers that even though people working for Breze take great pride in the brand, lately they have been unhappy with how the brand is being perceived in the market. A common grouse seems to be the customer service function, which seems to have let a great product down. She is told that it is difficult for customers to connect with the call centres for their service-related complaints because the call centres never have enough people to take the calls. Because of the heavy workload, attrition rate amongst the call centre employees is as much as 50 per cent. She is also informed by the HR team that they feel as if they are running on a treadmill, constantly trying to recruit employees for the call centre to replace the ones that keep leaving. This gives them no time for capability building. The customer service team tells her that the failure rate for Breze's air conditioners has risen over the last few years and the shortage of spares has led to delays in maintenance and repairs. The finance team complains about the sales team wanting to match their competitors' prices, which is leading to ever-reducing margins. The manufacturing team is unhappy as they are constantly being asked to bring down the cost of materials, which has led to key vendors refusing to deliver at such low prices. This has forced them to go back to vendors who have defaulted in the past and have been blacklisted by the company, since they are the only ones who agree to deliver raw materials at the reduced prices.

Armed with all this information, Nur decides to visit a couple of local markets to meet with their dealers. One dealer summarises the reason for the lower sales of Breze's ACs by saying, 'When a customer faces a problem with any product, they contact the dealer from whom they bought the product to get it fixed. They don't call the company's customer service number directly, even though post-sale service is required to be provided by the company. Lately, we have started receiving a lot of complaints from customers of your brand, much more than complaints about your competitors. Now, you tell me, if the price to the customer and the sales margin I get from your brand is the same as that of your competitors, then why wouldn't we urge customers to buy those products which are likely to get us the least number of complaints?'

Nur doesn't know how to counter this argument. She secretly agrees with what the dealer is saying.

Since their return to Malaysia, Nur and Adam have been invited by many of their friends and relatives to their houses for dinners and parties. Most of them have Breze ACs installed in their homes and offices. The conversation at such parties often veers towards how difficult it is to get a Breze AC serviced these days. They express a hope that now that Nur is heading the company, they won't have to jump through so many hoops anymore. Nur feels dismayed when she hears this but it adds to her determination to fix the problem as soon as she can.

Three weeks after her first meeting with her team members, Nur calls for another meeting with them to discuss everything she has discovered till then and to decide on a way forward. This is what she says:

'We were the leaders of this market because we offered the best-quality product, albeit at a price higher than the price we sell at today. Since then, new competitors have come in and slashed their prices to gain market share. In order to match their prices, we dropped ours too and have been dropping them ever since. The situation now is such that the entire industry lies bleeding. To maintain the low prices, everyone, including us and our competitors, has had to compromise on the quality of the products. Complaints are on the rise, and customers have started taking to social media to openly complain about all of us. The industry, in which we had managed to differentiate ourselves because of our quality, is now totally commoditised, just as coal, cement and steel are. Whoever offers the lowest price sells the most.

'We need to brainstorm collectively as a company and

agree upon one sustainable differentiator that will set us apart from the others. To be sustainable, the differentiator must arise from changes in our processes instead of merely being an announcement of change. I can also say upfront that our price cannot be the differentiator because it isn't easy to sustain the competitive advantage that comes from a lower price. Anyone can match a lower price within minutes. Our chosen sustainable differentiator should take a few months for us to implement and be very difficult for our competitors to copy. The differentiator can drive our agenda. We must all decide that we will put all our might behind it, we will invest time and effort to improve upon it continuously and we will never compromise on it, come what may.

'Having spoken to many of you, I have concluded that the problems we are facing are not caused by any shortcomings in the customer service department. On the contrary, it's the customer service people who are facing the brunt of problems that are originating in other departments of the company. Throwing more people at the customer service problem does not seem like a solution to me. Instead, we have to start ensuring that there are fewer problems with our products, hence fewer complaints from our customers.'

The team spends the rest of the day debating and rejecting various options for a suitable differentiator. Finally, they come up with a presentation whose first slide reads:

> Customers buy our ACs to cool their homes, not so that they have to repeatedly call our call centres. They call because our ACs have a problem. We will make sure that

> our products are defect-free so that the customers will have no reason to call us. And, in the rare event they need to, we will try to solve their problems in the least possible time. That will make us 'easy to deal with'. That can be our sustainable differentiator, our competitive advantage.

While Nur is pleased that the team has managed to identify a sustainable differentiator, she also knows that this will not be the end of their problems. To satisfy the requirements of their sustainable differentiator, Breze will need to identify metrics at each level that would indicate movement towards lower failure rates and faster recovery.

She decides to create a cross-functional task force that will identify the indicators of failure and recovery that will be tracked over time. While on the one hand this will help them prioritise what is important, on the other, it will tell them if they are making progress or not.

Over the next few months, the different departments get to work keeping the larger goal of their sustainable differentiator in mind. The first task is to ensure that every customer is able to reach them. Currently, 30 per cent of the incoming customer calls are abandoned due to shortage of manpower. At the next meeting of her team, Nur suggests that they outsource the work of customer service calls to external call centres, the employees of which can easily be trained to handle the complaints of Breze's customers.

The team is aghast when they hear about this idea. Breze

has always taken pride in the fact that they manage their call centres themselves. They feel that so far that has been their biggest differentiator vis-à-vis their competitors. By outsourcing customer service calls, Breze will be giving up its competitive edge. 'How can someone who doesn't work for Breze and handles customer calls of various brands empathise with our customers the way we do?' says someone in the room.

Nur argues that instead of spending their resources and energies in handling customer calls, which is a commoditised activity with little scope for making a difference as opposed to the others, Breze should differentiate itself from its competitors by coming up with a better designed service strategy, its own customised technology platform that is used by all outsourced partners and tighter quality control. In her opinion, a good service strategy comes before its efficient execution. If contracts with their service partners are tight, execution can be managed by effective supervision and by making their partners deliver what is expected of them.

She suggests they focus on building a platform on which their service partners can operate. This way, the functions of designing the service strategy, supervision of service partners and quality checks on them will remain within Breze. Outsourcing customer calls to external call centres will also rid Breze's HR team of the day-to-day pressures of recruiting new people to take customer calls.

Another team member pipes up quoting an article that said, 'Execution eats strategy for breakfast.'

Nur has a response to this too, 'Even the best execution in the whole world can't make a bad strategy work.' The final word from Nur shuts everyone up and there are no more protests.

Nur makes sure that a detailed plan is prepared to train the employees of external call centres to whom the task of taking customer calls has been outsourced. The course material for their training is created within Breze. It is mandatory that every external call centre employee taking customer calls is certified by a Breze employee before they are put behind a phone. The performance of every employee is monitored, and those found to be underperforming are taken off the calls, retrained and rostered only after recertification.

Now, when Nur attends social gatherings both within and outside of Breze, she hears murmurs of appreciation for the improvement in customer service at Breze. There are also a few discontented voices that feel even though the call centres are doing a great job, customer service in the field is still lagging. She is told of instances where repair jobs have been left incomplete by Breze technicians, forcing customers to call customer service repeatedly to get their problems resolved. Nur realises that until the service delivery function of Breze improves, the changes in customer service calls will not show an improvement.

Occasionally, while on field visits, Nur hears the opposite. Field service technicians complain about incomplete information being captured by call centres at the time of logging of complaints. Because the technicians receive incomplete information from the call centres about the actual problems being faced by customers, they often visit customers' homes with inadequate or wrong spare parts, forcing them to visit the customers' homes more than once. This leads to wastage of the technician's time as well as delay in the resolution of the problem faced by the customer. Nur is told that if the nature of the problem faced by the customer is captured correctly at the initial stage, the technician will carry the appropriate part and resolution will be faster.

When the head of the call centres resigns to take up another job, Nur merges the call centres and field service functions under one person—the current head of field service—and redesignates him as director of service. This stops any inter-departmental complaints because Breze now has an end-to-end service function that is responsible for both receiving customer complaints and resolving them at the field level.

In spite of receiving positive feedback for all the changes she has introduced in the company since joining, Nur is aware that unless product quality issues are resolved, the battle will remain only half won. She needs to understand why it is that the customers keep calling the call centres, why it is that they are facing so many problems with Breze air conditioners. Nur suggests that a bunch of senior management people listen in on the customer calls and read customer complaint emails for some time each day, so that a list of the problems being faced by Breze customers can be created.

A week of doing this throws up a list of ten issues that customers complain about the most.

'Is this all we could find? I'm sure there are more than ten reasons why our customers contact the call centres repeatedly to register complaints,' says Nur in the next team meeting.

'We went through every call that was received in the last month, and these were the only genuine problems we could discover from those calls. All other calls were because of some misunderstanding on the part of the customer,' replies the director of service.

'Meaning?'

'Many customers were calling because they either didn't know how to operate the AC or hadn't understood one of the AC's many features. These are not really complaints about problems with our ACs.'

'I see. If my children don't drink milk, despite my telling them it's good for them, it's not really their fault; it's mine. Maybe just saying that they should drink milk because it is healthy for them is not enough. Maybe I need to explain it to them in a manner that would appeal to them, such as saying that milk would help them become better at the sports they like playing,' says Nur.

'But the people who call us are not children. They're full-grown adults. They don't need that kind of handholding,' adds another team member.

'Remember, we had decided earlier that customers buy our

ACs to cool their homes, not so that they have to repeatedly get in touch with our call centres? Even if someone does not understand the features of our ACs, it is still our problem, not theirs. Are the people who've been listening to customer calls our older employees or our new hires?'

'It's a mix of employees.'

'Can we have only people who've been with us for less than three months listen to the calls, please? Chances of these people rationalising away the reasons for the call and blaming the customers would be lower.'

'Sure,' agrees the director of service.

Two weeks later, the new team comes up with a 250-point list of reasons why customers call Breze call centres.

Nur asks them to group together those items that may be arising from the same or similar problem. This brings the list down to forty-five items. At the next team meeting, they start brainstorming on these forty-five items, trying to drill down to the root cause of each one, which could be anything from the failure of a part, incorrect installation or untrained installer to the lack of sufficient information being provided to the customer. Having done this, against each issue, they list down the names of the divisions/functions that need to work together to get the issue fixed. They come up with forty-five cross-functional projects, each led by a team of three–four members, who are given a fixed timeline to address the problem.

Nur also announces that she and the division heads will review each of these forty-five projects once a month in two fortnightly batches, with five minutes dedicated to each project. Project teams are expected to come up with a single-page document that reports the progress against the deadline and lists any hurdles that they are facing.

The next few weeks prove to be eye-opening for everyone involved in this mammoth project. They discover some very interesting problems, and together they come up with some interesting—even out-of-the-box—solutions for them.

For instance, a frequent complaint was that Breze remotes only worked when they were brought quite close to the AC, whereas all other remotes at home, such as the ones for TVs, home theatres, etc., worked fine no matter how far you were from them. On further probing this problem, the concerned Breze team discovered that these days most devices at people's homes were using radio frequency (RF)-based remotes, which did not have to be pointed towards the device and could work over a larger range. Breze, on the other hand, was still using infra-red (IR)-based remotes that required the remote to be pointed at the AC from less than 10 yards. A simple switch from the IR to RF technology solved the problem of Breze remotes.

Another frequent complaint was that 30 per cent of the repairs to Breze conditioners required a revisit by the technician within a week. This problem has largely been addressed by merging the call centre and field visit divisions and bringing them under one departmental head. The team handling this issue soon realised there wasn't any one common reason for this repetitive failure; rather, it was different for every region. In some places, it was observed that not all technicians were equally capable of handling different sorts of problems. Often when a problem could not be fixed by one technician, a second visit was made by a more experienced technician. The team decided to organise training sessions for all technicians, where not only Breze officials conducted sessions but senior experienced technicians were also brought in to answer questions raised by novice technicians.

In areas where electrical fluctuation was common, the fuse provided in the AC units would often blow out whenever there was a surge of electric current. With the fuse blown, the power supply to the motor of the AC would turn off and the machine would be saved from damage. The team looking at mechanical issues realised that very often the only task that technicians performed in this area was to change the blown-out fuse of the AC unit. Even though Breze always provided two extra fuses with every AC unit enclosed in a small bag stapled to the instruction manual, most customers were unaware of their existence. The team found out that at the time of installation of the AC, customers were not being told about how to check if the AC's fuse had blown and how to replace the fuse themselves using the extra fuses provided with the unit. Training for the sales team was organised to ensure they conveyed the necessary information about fuses while selling the units. Thereafter, every time a customer called in with a complaint about the AC unit not working properly, the call centre would direct the customer, over the phone, to check if the fuse was blown and, if it was, to replace it with one of the extra fuses. This saved the technicians several field visits. Customers, too, were happy since they didn't need to wait for a technician to come fix their AC.

In this way, thirty out of the forty-five projects are completed successfully, because of which complaints from customers have also come down. Nur proves to be a supportive and understanding leader, who only ever looks irritated when she encounters a customer complaint caused by human error that could have been easily avoided. People working for her like the fact that she wants to make Breze a better company. They, too, start making whatever efforts they can to help her in her goal.

Nur often surfs social media apps to look for customer complaints—not only about Breze but also other brands and products in other categories. She decides to speak to the director of service about it.

'Why don't we have a separate team to handle complaints that are raised on social media sites by our customers?' asks Nur.

'Oh, usually those complaints are from people who are trolls, who just want to get into a slanging match on social media. We don't take what they say seriously. I don't think even half of them are our customers. They're just rabble-rousers.'

'I agree that some of the things written on social media about us are not polite. But sometimes even the people contacting our call centres or writing mails to us are not polite. Customers who are facing problems with our products and aren't able to resolve them are understandably frustrated. You can't expect them to be polite to us. We need to start addressing their problems instead of supressing or ignoring them.'

'Are you saying that we should create a separate customer service team to handle complaints that are posted on social media?' asks the director of service.

'Not just that. What you consider an adversity is actually an opportunity. We should try to have lower response times and recovery time targets for complaints received on social media versus the ones we get on call or mail.'

'Why so? Just because they are loud and impolite?'

'Have you noticed that people who complain about our ACs on social media are the same people who use social media to complain about many other companies, such as airlines and telecoms? They even complain about small things such as their toothpaste.'

'That's what I was saying. They are rabble-rousers. Habitual complainers.'

'Most companies have branded them that and, therefore, do not respond to them. If we do, we'll surprise them. And if we resolve their complaint in a timeframe they aren't expecting, then we'll shock them. I see this as an opportunity to convert some adversaries into supporters. If they are happy with us, they might even write nice things about us on social media, and that's the kind of advertising even money can't buy. Also, if we act differently from the other companies, it will make us stand out as a company that cares for its customers.'

'Okay, we can give this a trial run. What should we start with?'

'Let us target that we'll acknowledge a social media complaint within three minutes of it being posted and provide a solution for it in under an hour instead of our usual norm of four hours. Let's shock all of them!'

Within a few weeks, customers start posting salutary messages on social media about Breze's responsiveness to social media complaints and their quick service recovery times. A national newspaper writes about Breze, calling it a 'benchmark for customer-centricity'. Since Nur is the main person interviewed by the newspaper, she quickly comes into the public eye. Customers start tagging Nur every time they raise a complaint about Breze on social media.

The communications team advises Nur to shut down all her social media accounts. Paying no heed to their suggestion, Nur sets up alerts for her name on all social media apps instead. This way, she gets an instant alert whenever a customer tags her, and she is instantly able to forward the complaint to the service team for fast resolution.

The news of the CEO of a big company personally responding to complaints spreads far and wide. Nur is inundated with interview requests and one question pops up in all her interviews—how does she find the time to respond to each social media message personally while being responsible for running such a big company as Breze?

Nur usually responds by saying that the time and effort people spend on an activity is a function of how much it matters to them. If they find something to be of importance, they are more likely to give it the priority it deserves. She further mentions that since excellence of service is Breze's prime differentiator in a competitive market, everyone in Breze treats it as top priority. Once she even tells an interviewer with a laugh that forwarding eight to ten complaints in a day to her customer service team is nothing compared to the number of jokes she receives and forwards in her various WhatsApp groups. At an all-hands meeting of the company, she gives a talk on how if a brand wants to be customer-centric, its agenda has to be driven by more than the service division. Excellence in service is only possible if it is driven by the CEO and all the division heads in a collaborative manner.

Six months after Nur joins Breze, the COVID-19 pandemic strikes the world. In Malaysia, everyone is asked to stay indoors as much as possible. Call centres are shut, and technicians are not allowed to visit customer homes for repairs. It doesn't help that every member of the family is stuck indoors and, it being the onset of summer, ACs are required 24x7.

Nur knows that if urgent steps are not taken, the goodwill Breze has earned in the last few months will be lost. She, along with her team, decide that customer service agents will take customer calls from their homes. Breze asks all their call centre partners to ship a laptop to every agent taking a call on behalf of Breze. The IT team creates a platform to transfer calls to the agents' laptops so that they can take customer calls from homes easily. Within ten days of the declaration of the lockdown, Breze's customer service facilities are up and running, albeit from homes spread across the country.

Breze even launches its app during the first phase of the pandemic, allowing customers to book their complaints through the app. This leads to a reduction in customer calls since most people prefer to book complaints through the app.

The inability to visit customer homes forces Breze to figure out new ways in which to help customers carry out minor repairs on their own. Short videos on how to clean filters, mend fuses, remove drainage blocks, etc. are uploaded on YouTube, and often when a complaint is received, the customer is directed to these do-it-yourself videos. This proves to be a huge success because for small problems in their air conditioners, people prefer to carry out minor repairs on their own instead of allowing an outsider into their homes.

By the time the lockdown is lifted and normalcy is restored, the majority of the complaints are being received through the app and fewer people are calling in for minor repairs that they can do on their own. At the first physical Monday meeting that they have in months, Nur comments, 'I wonder why we needed a pandemic to do for the customer what we should have done in any case. Let us not go back to our earlier ways. I think we should make all our processes pass the COVID test, that is, let us assume that the pandemic isn't over, that we must manage everything from our homes in remote locations, and then come up with solutions.'

At the end of the first year of Nur joining Breze, reports show that sales have gone up significantly. In the next two years, Breze becomes the market leader once again. Every employee, dealer and partner feels proud of what they have achieved together.

At a company get-together held to celebrate the regained market leadership, Nur proudly says, 'We do not sell cola or candies, something that customers can try for themselves and discard if they don't like the taste. Air conditioners are expensive and they are an investment. When someone wants to buy one, they usually check with three other people before doing so to find out their experience. It could be a neighbour, a colleague from work or even the AC dealer. And if any of these people shares a bad opinion about our ACs, then most probably the customer will not buy from us. Hence, our real advertisements are not those that are played on the TV or printed in newspapers. Our best ads are the testimonies of customers who are satisfied with what they are using. Our service is our biggest salesperson.'

On one of her subsequent trade visits to Penang, Nur asks a dealer which AC they sold the most and what is the reason for that.

The dealer replies, 'When a customer faces product failure,

they contact the dealer from whom they bought the AC, despite knowing the phone number of the company. Your price to the customer and margin for us is the same as that of your competitors. All things being equal, I am more likely to sell the AC that gets me the least complaints.'

Nur realises that this is like what she heard from another dealer a few years ago, when she had just joined Breze. The only difference is that this time the dealer is talking about urging more people to buy Breze ACs because the dealer receives the least number of complaints for them.

Here are some statements that you should respond to for the business that you are a part of, as an owner or a manager. Remember to respond honestly.

The statements must be answered in a yes/no format. If there are any statements that are not relevant to your business, put a cross against them.

- ☐ Customers have multiple means of reaching us to register their complaints and convey their feedback.
- ☐ We capture the feedback of every customer at every customer touchpoint. We study this feedback to reduce customer complaints.
- ☐ We have identified the top ten reasons why our customers call our customer service centre with complaints and have project teams working on a targeted reduction of calls due to each of these causes.

- ☐ Because of the efforts of our project teams, a smaller proportion of customers are contacting us with complaints, and our service recovery time is also reducing with every passing month.
- ☐ We have significantly lower response and recovery times for complaints received via social media.
- ☐ The majority of our customers do not contact us with the same complaint within the same month.
- ☐ The customer's previous contact history is available on the screens of customer-facing teams while they attend their calls.
- ☐ While we outsource customer service to external call centres, we never outsource the design and quality checks.
- ☐ The senior management team of the customer service division has people with experience in other customer-facing commercial roles.
- ☐ We have standard specs for staff hired by our partner call centres and each person being hired by our partners is first vetted by us.

Now consider the statements to which you have responded with a 'No'. Discuss and reflect on these within your company, read more about **service strategy** and/or ask some experts about how to apply these statements to your specific case.

Doing this could help you differentiate your business from that of your competitors. Permanently.

5

SETTING UP SHOP ON JUPITER'S MOON

Reaching customers effectively and efficiently

It is minus 11 degrees in Alaska on the morning of 8 January 2081, when Ron walks towards the chamber in which his body will get converted to energy, only to be reconverted back into a body once he reaches Europa. With a surface temperature of minus 160 degrees, Europa—one of the ninety-five moons of Jupiter and almost 400 million miles away from Earth—is expected to be much colder than Alaska.

Today is a big day at the Alaska Tele Transport Station (TTS), as Ron is the one millionth human to be tele-transported to Europa. The atmosphere at the station is one of jubilation, with buntings and balloons hanging all around the centre and a band playing jaunty music. Hundreds of virtual cameras are suspended mid-air, capturing the event at every step, from every angle.

Thirty years ago, Europa was identified as a habitable colony for humanity—a place for the human race to take refuge in and not perish like the dinosaurs—in case a large meteor ever hit Earth. Though living conditions on Europa are far from comfortable for humans, it is the only spot in the entire universe with adequate oxygen in the atmosphere, which is why it was selected all those years ago despite its distance from Earth.

The first hundred-odd humans who were taken to Europa endured a rocket journey of three years before they could land. In the last thirty years, success rates for tele-transportation, which was being tested for decades, have reached near perfection. You now enter an evacuation chamber, where your body and belongings are converted into a light beam and then transmitted, almost 400 million miles away, to a receiving station on Europa. You travel at the speed of light and voila, in thirty-five minutes the light beam that was you is received by a large antenna on Europa, transmitted to a receiving chamber and then reconstructed back to your original form.

In the process of energisation and reconstruction, some deliberate cellular modifications are made to the human body for it to withstand temperatures as low as minus 200 degrees and for the lungs to perform their function at relatively low oxygen levels. Europa has one-seventh of Earth's gravity, which is why feet and legs are also partially modified to resemble those of a kangaroo, allowing a person to hop on Europa instead of walking. There has been a protracted debate on this subject for years because many individuals and organisations are against genetic modification. The debate was finally settled with an overriding condition that such changes will be allowed only for humans migrating to Europa.

Over the last twenty years that TTSs located at different parts of Earth have been beaming humans to Europa, a handful of climate-controlled interconnected villages have come up there. These villages have been built a few metres below Europa's surface, which is largely composed of ice-like mountains, some almost 60 miles tall. Hydrogen is available in plenty in Europa's atmosphere and is used to heat and run homes, malls, cinemas, offices, factories and cars. The initial lot of food supplies, building materials and automobiles were transported from Earth on rockets. However, once the TTSs were up and running, and as the tele-transportation process became more efficient, the 'Europisation' of manufacturing started. Everything that was required on Europa was produced on large 3D printers, which only needed a design to come up with a product as good as the one on Earth. Large printing factories, warehouses and office complexes were a part of most villages and mostly employed people living in the nearby village.

In the case of most villages, it was noticed that in the early days of settlement, the shops would store hardware, home décor, furniture and appliances. Once the village had enough people and houses were built and decorated, the same shops would change their line of business and start selling food, clothes and other consumables. This pattern was seen, without any deviation, in village after village as the population of Europa grew.

After seven days of acclimatisation on Europa, Ron is taken to the induction centre where his predesignated role awaits him. Considering his professional experience on Earth, he has been assigned the role of heading the apparel and accessories division of an organisation that procures goods from various factories and makes them available for sale at stores across Europa. Ron's division sells clothes, belts, shoes, watches, sunglasses, etc. to both small and large stores.

Next, he meets his team to understand the products and the profile of their sellers and buyers. The apparel team has been doing great thanks to the fast-growing population, selling almost everything as fast as the printers print them. However, the same cannot be said about the accessories team, which is struggling to meet its sales targets. In accessories, while watches have been selling well, other products have not been able to meet even 50 per cent of the planned sales.

To familiarise himself with the selling process and to gain important customer insights, Ron decides to spend the next few days visiting stores across different villages. Most stores in malls are large-format stores comprising two to four floors each, where one can buy anything—clothes, accessories, linen, home décor, furniture and food. In addition to these large stores, which are mainly located in malls, and there is one large mall for every five to six villages, Ron also visits some standalone specialised stores located within the villages, which sell single-category products. On probing, he discovers what is a relatively recent phenomenon, with the number of small, specialised, standalone stores increasing with the growth in population.

He also notices that while accessories are well-stocked in most small stores, the variety is rather scanty in large stores. For instance, where a standalone sunglasses store will have at least forty or fifty different types of frames available in each shape and size, a big departmental store displays only ten-odd styles. He finds that the same is true for watches, belts and wallets as well.

On one such day full of store visits, Ron and a colleague stop for lunch at a fast food restaurant around mid-day. A person, who on Earth would be of South Asian origin, sits at the table next to them and smiles at Ron when their eyes meet. They start talking. His name is Mahesh, and he, too, has arrived in Europa a couple of weeks ago. He lives in the village next to Ron's on Europa. On Earth, he was a distributor of films to movie theatres in India. The discussion circles around their mutual love for movies and the challenges that both are facing after their move to Europa. After almost an hour, Ron gets up to leave. He and Mahesh tap on each other's watches to exchange their contact details, promising each other to stay in touch.

Ron feels a bit awkward while walking, rather hopping, out of the restaurant. He is getting used to this new style of moving from one place to another, but his shins hurt from all the hopping. However, his embarrassment is short-lived as he can see other people hopping from one place to another, some of them looking as uncomfortable as him.

The very next day, Ron receives a call from Mahesh, who suggests they go out for drinks and dinner at an Indian restaurant called Mehfil he has discovered near his home. Since Ron is fond of spicy Indian food, he agrees. He realises that this will also be a great opportunity for him to find out more about how other newcomers to Europa are faring.

They meet up outside Mehfil and hop into the restaurant together. Once they are seated, the conversation flows smoothly over aam panna mojitos and appetisers like chicken tikka and malai paneer. As the evening progresses, Ron discovers that Mahesh is the same age as him and, despite growing up in distinctly different countries and milieus, they share a similar outlook on life. Maybe what they say about people of a certain generation having similar expectations from life is true.

'Mahesh, what work have you been assigned here in Europa? asks Ron.

'I was in the films distribution business in India, hence I've been asked to do the same work here.'

'Oh wow! I like Indian movies. Your superstars like Shahbaz Khan and Rohit Kapoor are magnificent. I really enjoy all the singing and dancing that is a part of Indian movies.'

'Ron, you are talking about Hindi films. Hindi is spoken in large parts of the country. But I was distributing films in a different language, Telugu. Telugu is the most spoken language in one state in the southern part of India called Andhra Pradesh.'

'Oh! So Telugu movies are not a part of Bollywood then? Was yours a small, niche business then?'

'On the contrary, Tollywood, as the Telugu film industry is popularly called, is as large as Bollywood. While only 6 per cent of Indians speak Telugu, movies made in this language contribute to 18 per cent of movies made in India. In contrast, 45 per cent of Indians speak Hindi. However, Hindi movies contribute to only 22 per cent of movies made in India.'

'That's a huge gap. Why is that? Are Telugu language movies that good?' asks Ron.

'I don't think it has that much to do with the quality of films as it has to do with their distribution. Andhra Pradesh has twenty-eight movie screens per million people while the rest of India has only six screens per million people. The easy availability of screens in Andhra Pradesh makes movie-watching convenient and tempts more people to go to the theatre. This has led to a disproportionate consumption of films in Telugu.'

'That makes complete sense. Why isn't the rest of the country following this example?'

'I guess this is another case of "not invented here",' replies Mahesh.

'And has it always been this way?'

'Yes, I'm told that it's been like this for the last hundred years. Even though, over the years, newspapers and magazines have written off large screens several times because of the feeling that the ease of watching movies on home theatre and OTT streaming channels would destroy the theatre-going habit of the people. But movie-watching in theatres has only grown.'

'So are you trying to replicate the Tollywood model in Europa?'

'Yes, that's why I was brought here. Not that people are not watching movies here—they are. However, most people prefer to rent movies and watch them in the comfort of their homes. Going out to watch a movie is not considered a family or a social outing in Europa. But the authorities here feel that when people go to watch a movie in a theatre, especially to one that is located in a mall, they also end up spending money on food, drinks, other shopping etc., which is all good for business. My job is to increase the number of screens in Europa so that people are tempted to get out of their homes and go the theatre.'

'And what kind of a target is that?'

'One cinema screen in every village and more than one in every mall.'

Ron enjoys the evening, and not just for the delicious food and the engaging conversation. He realises that the insight that making your product available at more places can increase consumption can be a gamechanger for his business too. On the way back home, his mind starts working on the various action points his business can work on to adapt to this model.

By the time he reaches home, he has figured out the data he wants his team to gather to support a plan that is taking shape in his head. He opens the Format Generator on his watch, projects the screen from his watch to his bedroom wall and stares at the app long enough for it to convert his thoughts into multiple data formats. Then, he selects the relevant ones and stores them to be shared with his teams tomorrow.

Next morning, he shares these formats with his teams and asks them to fill out the blank spaces with information about the number of shops in every village that stock their apparel and accessory lines. He asks them to follow this up by identifying the villages where sales per 1,000 population is the highest for each apparel and accessory line.

Once the data is entered in these formats, it becomes clear that villages with more shops stocking a line of products have more sales per 1,000 residents. The teams agree that 'shops per 1,000 population' is the right metric to compare the sales of each product line. They calculate this for each product category, giving them a clear picture of which villages require more shops for each product line. Ron gives the sales team thirty days to increase the shops stocking their products to fill the distribution gap in every village for each product line.

From past experience, the sales team knows that placing a product in the market and making sure the shopkeepers start selling it takes at least four to five visits from them, spread over four weeks. Shopkeepers need to see a salesperson's face at least three or four times in quick succession to be convinced that they will be adequately serviced if they start selling the product. Since one salesperson can visit only three or four shops per day, the sales team realises that if they do as Ron has asked and try to place their products in the targeted number of shops, it will take them at least 180 days, even 240 days, to complete this task. There is no way they can do this within thirty days. They decide that the solution to this problem lies in taking the alternate route, and they double the size of the sales team. If more trained salespeople can be requisitioned from Earth, they might be able to complete the assigned task within sixty days and have the resources to provide the long-term service that the larger number of shops will need.

Ron agrees to this plan and goes to meet the Europan resources head, whose job is to identify skill gaps on Europa and requisition humans with the necessary experience from Earth, to ask for more people to join the sales function of his business. In his heart, he is confident that the task of boosting distribution can be completed in the targeted number of days because they have approached the problem with a data-driven solution, rather than just relying on a wish sprinkled with a generous dose of bravado.

That night Ron meets his mother in his living room on a Holocall. Ron's parents are farmers in Colorado and grow potatoes in the 500-odd acres of farmland they own. This year, they plan to switch some of their holdings to growing corn instead of potatoes, as the former is easier to grow. His mother tells him about how they have hand-picked some of their best farm hands and moved them to corn farming. Ron does not agree with that decision. He feels that given that potatoes are a relatively more difficult crop to grow, his parents should have kept the best people for potato farming. His mother's argument is that the processes for growing potatoes are well-established on their farm, whereas corn is something they have never grown before, therefore it is better to have more experienced hands in corn farming at the start, at least until they have set up processes for that too.

After the call, Ron thinks about what his mother said for a long time. He realises that there might be some logic in what she was saying, so he decides to pull out his best salespeople from the apparel division and move them to the accessories division. This move makes those who have been moved unhappy because in the business, apparel is considered to be a superior division to accessories. Ron takes the time to meet all these people and explains to them how the need of the hour is creation—filling the distribution gap—and not maintenance, that is servicing existing clients. Therefore, it is important for the best people to move to accessories. This satisfies the team, who feel honoured to be singled out as being the best.

A week later, Mahesh and Ron meet again at a different Indian restaurant, Tandoor. Ron tells him about how Mahesh's example of screen density increasing consumption inspired him to scientifically set up new distribution goals for the products in his own business. Mahesh is happy to hear that he was able to help Ron, but seems preoccupied with a problem of his own. Mahesh's company has decided to insource the catering work in the cinemas owned by them, with the objective of adding food and beverage (F&B) revenues to their sales. This means that Mahesh is now in charge of a larger business and of a more varied team. But this change is not something Mahesh is too pleased with because on Earth, he observed that adding F&B business to the film distribution business never did well. This is why in Europan villages, F&B at cinemas has been outsourced from the very beginning. Mahesh feels that it will be an onerous task to boost F&B sales in addition to ticket sales, which are growing slower than expected.

While Mahesh is explaining his problem to Ron, the waiter arrives to take the order. Mahesh is familiar with the restaurant and places an order for chicken tikka masala and garlic naan without even looking at the menu and turns back to continue his conversation. But the waiter interrupts them to suggest that they would be better off adding raita, a curd dish, to the meal, which will help in cutting the spice of the chicken, making it more palatable for Ron. Mahesh nods in agreement, continuing his conversation with Ron. The waiter interrupts them again and suggests that they could order a salad too, since they haven't ordered any vegetables with the meal. At this second interruption, Ron sees Mahesh lose his cool. His fists are clenched and the lines on his forehead have become more pronounced too. Mahesh turns to the waiter in anger and snaps at him to bring the salad and any other dish that the waiter thinks will be good for their appetite and health. Realising that he has been very rude, Mahesh takes a deep breath and tries to give the waiter a conciliatory smile. Then he says, 'You know who you remind me of? My mother.' Both Ron and Mahesh break out into a loud laughter, while the waiter smiles as he walks away towards the kitchen.

In the next moment, Mahesh becomes serious again. Scratching his head, he says to Ron, 'Hang on. Do you think this waiter has a sales target for add-on items like salads, side dishes, beverages and desserts? Otherwise, why would he push so hard for them? It's not like he's so concerned about my health, after all, he's not my fricking mother, is he?'

Ron nods his head contemplatively.

Mahesh continues, 'This waiter just gave me an idea. Why don't I set similar targets for my ticket sales staff to encourage them to start upselling F&B at the cinema?'

Ron, too, is struck by an idea. It is not enough to simply make more accessories available in a greater number of shops for sales to increase. The sales team will have to upsell the accessories and for that they will need to be trained on creating stylish combinations of clothes and accessories for different occasions. This way, those buying apparel can also be tempted into buying matching accessories with it. Ron closes his eyes to bring up his virtual to-do list on his glasses and bats his eyelids a few times to make a note that he has to discuss this idea with his team tomorrow morning. While he is doing this, the aroma of piping hot, spicy chicken tikka masala hits his nose. The waiter is standing behind them, smiling, ready to serve their meal. His eyes point towards the napkins suggestively, indicating that they should cover their shirts to protect them from the rich gravy. Mahesh looks at the waiter, nods and says, 'Yes, Mom,' as he tucks the napkin under his shirt collar with a wide grin.

Next morning, Ron goes to meet the Europan resources head once again and asks him for help in sourcing fashion experts who can teach his sales teams on how to match apparel with accessories like bags, watches, glasses, etc. In turn, his salespeople will train their colleagues in various stores on how to upsell apparel and accessories. Ron's experience on Earth has taught him that salespersons armed with a good technique are more confident with customers and end up selling more. This confidence in selling also makes them enjoy their jobs more, reducing the attrition rate of salespersons in stores.

Three months later, Ron's team has successfully delivered on the distribution targets he set for them, and sales of accessories are much higher than planned. Much has happened in his personal life, too, since then. A week after dinner at Tandoor, Mahesh introduced Ron to his colleague Hiba, who is from Sudan. Hiba moved to Europa a year ago and oversees visual merchandising and displays in Mahesh's team. This first meeting resulted in a fierce argument between them. Ron happened to mention that he thought advertising was a waste of money since increased sales was the result of heavy lifting done by salespeople inside stores rather than advertising. This got Hiba all riled up, and she took Ron to task for saying something she clearly thought was idiotic. That day, they parted ways still angry with each other. But they both also realised that there was something they liked about the other, so when Ron asked Hiba to meet again, she readily agreed. It took them two more meetings to realise it was better to 'agree to disagree' on certain issues. They were also able to recognise and appreciate each other's intellectual and emotional sides. Soon they became inseparable, and a month ago, Hiba moved in with Ron.

Life has changed for both of them since that day. Ron, who rarely cooks at home and eats out on most days, is now sharing a home with Hiba, who makes elaborate meals at home, being extremely particular about what she eats. Ron is messy and leaves his things all around the house. Hiba, on the other hand, is a neat-freak and likes to keep her home tidy and clean. Eventually, Ron gives in to Hiba's style of living since he realises that the order that Hiba brings to his otherwise bohemian lifestyle is good for him.

Hiba loves visiting unknown small shops in faraway villages. She goes to these shops based on recommendations from her friends and buys foods she considers healthy, even though they are being sold at a premium. Ron often compares the ingredients on the food she buys with those that are available in supermarkets. Most of the time, he doesn't find any difference between them, except for the fact the food she buys is homemade, produced in small quantities and packed by hand. This justifies the higher cost of these products vis-à-vis mass-produced products.

Ron doesn't complain about this to Hiba. Instead, he shows these products to his product managers, asking them to do something similar. He asks them to come up with variants of their existing products, which will have only minor differences from the original products. These products will be produced in small lots, carry a different brand name and they won't be sold through the same stores that stock their regular products. Ron challenges his sales team to think of different and untried ways to make their new products reach customers.

The sales guys come up with many new ideas, such as door-to-door marketing where salespeople go to customers' homes, carrying limited stocks with them, allowing the customers to try apparel and accessories in the comfort of their homes. Another idea they come up with is that of appointment-shopping, where large stores are stocked with limited merchandise and customers visit only by appointment. They also throw up the idea of starting boutiques inside people's homes. All these ideas are targeted towards making the product seem more personalised, allowing Ron's business to charge a premium for them. To check their viability, Ron puts together a roadmap to implement each of these ideas and any more ideas that the sales team come up with in the future.

Over the next few weeks, Ron and the sales team observe that each one of the new personalised channels is delivering more sales than expected, and even though the sales numbers are a fraction of the sales from large stores, the profit margins on these designer products are good. Also, those designer products that do well in a successful season can then be mass-produced in the next season to be sold through the large stores.

The flywheel keeps turning well and the business keeps growing. The rapid growth means Ron needs to regularly hire more people to man the new stores, service the distribution channels and fill the gaps created by salespeople leaving for other jobs. But there just aren't enough people on Europa to meet the demand. Ron once jokes with Hiba that at the rate they are growing, soon half the village will be buying from his stores while the other half will be selling there. And if that happens, who will watch movies at Hiba's theatres? Hiba laughs at the joke but knows that Ron is concerned about the growing need for manpower. She suggests to him that he should outsource the hiring and supervision of salespeople to a human resources organisation. She knows of such a firm headed by her friend, Sue, and has outsourced to them the staffing for their F&B outlets too.

The next day, Ron connects with Sue over email. They agree upon the commercials and Ron transfers all details of the salespeople on his rolls to Sue's company. In their contracts, they have included enough penalty clauses to ensure that Ron never falls short of sales staff.

Ron is now free to focus on creating new products and experimenting with new sales channels. The business launches many new products in the following quarter and experiments with new sales channels, too, something which was put on hold for a while because of the shortage of salespeople. Even though Ron has managed to solve the manpower problem, there is something else that is causing him concern. Sales are dropping across all categories, and the number of product returns from customers has increased. The drop is not consistent with the market because Ron's competitors are continuing to boom. The cost of selling, which Ron personally monitors weekly to ensure that enough work is done to keep it under check, has also started ballooning as the unit sales have gone down. His boss suggests that to control costs, they should let go of some salespeople they have recently hired. But Ron is clear in his head that downsizing is not the best solution to this problem, as this might lead to an even bigger drop in sales, leading to a downward spiral, which will be very difficult to overcome.

Next weekend, Ron asks Hiba to visit five stores where his products sold as a customer. Hiba goes to the stores, walks around in the aisles, touches some products, carries a few to the trial room and asks the salesperson for more details about the available sizes, colours, etc. In the evening, she comes back and gives the full report to Ron, but she has nothing positive to say about her experience. According to her, salespeople were difficult to find in the store—instead of tailing her through the aisles, most of them kept their distance. When she showed interest in a product, the salesperson had nothing to say about the options available in the store, nor did they show her other products in the same category or suggest an accessory to go with the product. They quietly rung up the product she chose, put it in a bag and handed it to her.

Ron is surprised when he hears this. After all, their entire business model depends on the salespersons doing their job efficiently. Ron believes that salespeople can make a huge difference to the outcome of a sale if they take personal initiative. It is to ignite this initiative that companies link incentives with sales. Some salespeople make almost 50 per cent of their income by meeting targets and getting incentives, allowing them to earn 30–40 per cent more than their colleagues who are not paying attention to customers and hence are not getting these incentives. On the question of incentives for salespeople, Ron has faced a lot of opposition from people of similar ranks who belong to other divisions of the business. He has been accused of being discriminatory in favour of salespeople since his own background is that of sales. Ron usually pacifies them by saying, 'Your work profile is very different from that of salespeople. You chose certainty over chance; salespeople don't do that. Also, bear in mind that if a salesperson misses their target, they take home 20–30 per cent less than what you do, after putting in the same effort as you.'

That is why Ron is so disturbed by what Hiba has told him.

The next morning, he asks three of the highest-performing salespeople working in his stores to come visit him in his office. These people were earlier on the rolls of Ron's business but lately have been transferred to Sue's firm. The boys seem very pleased to meet Ron after a long time and chat freely over coffee and cookies. After the initial exchange of news about their families and the weather, Ron asks them about their experience with the new firm.

Initially, they seem hesitant to say anything. However, a bit of probing from Ron gets them talking. They tell him that Sue, to whom Ron has outsourced hiring and supervision of the sales teams, has failed to strike a balance between various functions. She has also capped all sales incentives to 10 per cent of a person's salary, which is why there is a lack of initiative amongst the salespeople. The salespeople realise that regardless of how much effort they make with a customer, they will earn only 10 per cent more than what they earn by just being present on the floor and answering only those questions that the customer asks. They feel that there is no need for them to exert themselves if the returns are going to be so poor. They also tell Ron that Sue has been filling vacancies by hiring people with little or no prior sales experience to keep wages low and that she has made the training sessions shorter by a couple of days to save costs.

Ron realises that outsourcing his salespeople, lock stock and barrel, to another firm was a mistake that has to be reversed. He should have retained a small sales team within his company to perform strategy development and quality check functions. The remaining functions could then have been outsourced to Sue.

On the drive back home that evening, Ron listens to songs sung by Saria Wail, a Sudanese singer Hiba has introduced to him. The soothing music playing in the background allows Ron to isolate the real problems that came up in that day's discussions from the angst he has been feeling lately because of the low sales numbers.

He decides to meet Sue tomorrow morning to ask her to transfer back to his payroll four of his best salespeople. Their job will include strategy development and quality control. This small team will have to make sure that the compensation structure of salespeople has enough juice to bring out individual initiative. They will also ensure that adequate training of personnel is being carried out and only those who perform well in training are certified to become salespersons for Ron's business. He realises that in addition to money, people also need to see growth prospects for themselves, and a hope of getting into a strategy role within the parent company will drive that.

At home, over dinner and dessert—baseema, a traditional Sudanese cake that Hiba has baked herself, without sugar of course—Ron tells Hiba about everything he learnt that day. He also tells her that staying in touch with ground realities is most critical for a business so that it can assess the ever-changing opportunities and adapt to them with new processes, structures and policies.

Here are some statements that you should respond to for the business that you are a part of, as an owner or a manager. Remember to respond honestly.

The statements must be answered in a yes/no format. If there are any statements that are not relevant to your business, put a cross against them.

- ☐ We have estimated the number of customer contact points required to meet our sales targets based on population and population density.
- ☐ We have set up upsell and cross-sell targets for our salespeople, and the level of these is raised every year.
- ☐ Salespeople are equipped with leads and are trained by experts to identify upsell/cross-sell opportunities.
- ☐ We have multiple sales channels and have dedicated, trained manpower for each of these channels.
- ☐ We have experimented with a new sales channel in the last one year.
- ☐ We have stated specifications for the staff to be hired by our exclusive distribution partners, and they are trained and certified by us before they are allowed to work in the stores.
- ☐ We deploy distribution resources of superior quality and in larger numbers in areas where our market share or the penetration of our products is low.
- ☐ At least 30 per cent of the income of our frontline staff is linked to their performance.
- ☐ The productivity of our distribution staff has risen quarter on quarter in the last year.

- ☐ We calculate the cost of sales for every channel and ensure that it reduces every year.

Now consider the statements to which you have responded with a 'No'. Discuss and reflect on these within your company, read more about **distribution strategy** and/or ask some experts about how to apply these statements to your specific case.

Doing this could help you build and run a distribution network that delivers sustained sales growth.

6

TOUCHING CUSTOMERS' HEARTS

Creating a brand that connects

It is 8.15 a.m. and Kobby is waiting outside his boss Addae's house in Abelemkpe, a posh neighbourhood of Accra, Ghana. In all the time that Kobby has known Addae, the latter has never stepped out a minute before or after 8.20 a.m. on the days he has to go to work. As expected, the main door of the bungalow opens at 8.20 a.m. sharp and Addae steps out dressed in a navy-blue Italian suit with a bright green Ferragamo tie. The rhythmic clicks of the heels of his patent leather Bally shoes sound the same as they had when Kobby first started driving Addae to work some twenty years ago.

Kobby straightens his cap, rushes to the rear door of the car and opens it for Addae, who nods and smiles at Kobby and slides into the back seat. Kobby gently shuts the door, rushes across to the front of the car to get in, fastens his seat belt and drives out of the long driveway towards the city centre.

Addae is usually on the phone during the twenty-minute drive to work that takes them via Olusegan Obasanjo Wat, to Achimota Road, Hilla Limann Highway and finally to Barnes Road, where the office building is located. He usually uses this time to catch up with one of his vice presidents, a different one each day.

Addae was the head of a local bank that had its presence in Accra and in the states that run alongside Ghana's border with neighbouring Toga. A year ago, his bank merged with another bank from Savannah, which had a strong presence in the states bordering Cote D'Ivoire. While both banks were small players and did not have enough infrastructure to match the large banks of Ghana, the consensus was that the merged entity would provide an opportunity for building a larger bank with national presence, something that could compete with the other big banks in Ghana.

Addae is well-known in industry circles because of the active role he plays in several industry associations headquartered in Accra. His reputation made him the natural choice to head the new bank, which was named 'Your Ghana Bank' or YGB. The management of the new bank consists of an equal number of senior members from both the merging banks. Many critics of the deal, who were sceptical of YGB's ability to succeed as a big bank, said, 'Two puppies can only make a big noise, not a big dog.' But Addae is pretty sure that if they think differently and execute smartly, they can make YGB big—bigger than the sum of all its parts.

This morning, Addae is on the speaker phone with his VP of marketing, who is responsible for the brand-building of the new bank. The VP is suggesting that they should go big on advertising to make sure that the YGB name is on everyone's minds and lips in Ghana, after which getting potential customers to open their accounts or transact with YGB will be a cakewalk.

But Addae doesn't see it that way. He argues that they first need to conduct research on what it is that most customers want from their banks. With that research in hand, they need to assess whether YGB can deliver on those expectations. If not, then before starting a huge advertising campaign, YGB needs to build the requisite infrastructure and incorporate the processes that will provide the services that customers expect from their bank.

Addae also expresses his displeasure with the marketing folks of today, who tend to find the solution to every problem in an advertising campaign. He says to his VP, 'Building a brand takes more than shooting a thirty-second ad film.'

The VP responds with, 'But, Addae, building infrastructure and incorporating processes is not the job of the marketing guys. That needs to be done by the operations team. We can only try to sell what we have currently.' The car is nearing the office now, so Addae closes the conversation with the VP by saying, 'A brand is known by what a brand does and how it behaves, just as people are. Let us slot some time over the next couple of days to continue this conversation.' The VP of marketing agrees and hangs up the phone.

Outside the office, Kobby quickly gets out of the car, goes across and opens the door on Addae's side. Addae responds to Kobby's smile with a grateful nod as he steps out of the car and swiftly climbs the six steps that lead to the lobby.

It is late that evening when Kobby gets back home after dropping Addae to his house. His wife, Jojo, and son, Ekow, are waiting to have dinner with him. Kobby washes up, changes his clothes and sits down with them as Jojo serves a pot of waakye with a side of fried plantain.

While eating, Kobby looks at Ekow, who has a perturbed expression on his face. Ekow didn't do well at school because his focus was always more on sports than on studies. He played football for his school, which got him an admission and a scholarship to a college. However, the competition for getting into the college football team was intense and Ekow didn't make the cut. That left Ekow despondent. When Ekow suggested that academics wasn't his strong suite and that it would be better if he started a small business of his own, Kobby agreed with his son. Ekow dropped out of college and Kobby constructed a small room at the back of their house, from where Ekow could sell snack foods and basic provisions to the busy neighbourhood they lived in. The small shop does decent business, with people from the neighbourhood frequenting it for their daily needs. It keeps Ekow busy though, with travelling to the wholesale market every morning, interacting with customers during the day, updating the shop's accounts and making a list of things to be bought the next day. In the last six months that Ekow has been running the shop, he has learnt a lot, like understanding what products appeal most to customers, where he can purchase these products at low prices and how to negotiate with wholesale dealers for credit.

After dinner, Kobby suggests that they go for a walk to get some fresh air. Ekow agrees, and father and son start strolling quietly in the lane near their house. Initially, no one says a word, but Kobby, realising that something is troubling his son, gently probes him.

'Son, I can see something is bothering you. Why don't you tell me what's on your mind?' asks Kobby.

'It's nothing, Dad. For a few weeks now, I have been thinking that I want more than just a shop at the back of our house. I am young and hardworking, and I have a lot of ideas. And I have learnt the art of buying and selling in the last six months. I think I'm ready to scale up. What I would like is to open an independent grocery store on the main street that leads into our colony.'

'Ekow, I'm not denying that you have learnt a great deal from your stint as a shopkeeper; no doubt you have developed a keen eye to discern what customers want and what they don't. But selling a limited set of products from a small shop that caters to the needs of a small neighbourhood is very different from having a large grocery store in the main market that will need to attract customers from beyond the neighbourhood.' Recalling the conversation he overheard in the car that morning between Addae and his VP of marketing,

Kobby adds, 'You first need to find out why a customer chooses one particular grocery store and not the other. What is it that makes one grocery store a regular choice for a customer? Is it just proximity to where they live or is it more? You have to ask yourself if you know what makes a good grocery store brand and if you have it in you to become one. I think you should speak to a few people already in the business as well as to potential customers, and work towards building a brand for yourself before investing in a shop on the main street.'

The expression on Ekow's face, as Kobby is saying all this, is one of confusion. His eyes seem to be asking Kobby why he is deliberately trying to put roadblocks in the way of what Ekow thinks is a great idea. But all Ekow says is, 'Dad, I want to be a grocer, a storekeeper, not start a company. Why do I need to think about building a brand?' Sensing Ekow's disappointment, Kobby tries to reassure him by saying, 'That's not true, son. Every person needs to think of their brand. Only then can they get customers to trust them. Think about what brand you want to build for yourself, and we will talk about this again when you are ready with that answer.'

A week later, Kobby is driving Addae to his office, and Addae is once again on a call with his VP of marketing. Kobby overhears the conversation. The VP has apparently carried out a customer survey, which has shown that, amongst other things, customers want their bank to have a lot of branches so that there is a branch close by no matter where they live.

The customers have also mentioned that they do not like the bank to charge them fees for transactions and that they want the bank to pay a fair interest rate for their deposits. They would also like their banking problems to be resolved without too much hassle. Based on the survey, the VP suggests that YGB should consider opening at least 200 more branches to match the number of branches the largest bank has. He also thinks that YGB should engage a football star as the bank's brand ambassador, since the two largest banks have film stars endorsing them. Kobby smiles to himself, knowing what Addae will say to this suggestion.

'Yes, we have an ambition to grow but that doesn't mean we will open 200 branches just because the largest bank has them. We cannot go around replicating what a bank ten times our size does. I respect a customer's expectations of their bank, but we need to find other ways of providing them services close to their home instead of opening so many branches. One idea that comes to mind is finding ways to reduce the number of interactions that a customer needs to have with their bank. What I mean to say is that our services should be such that customers are not required to visit the bank too often. This way the customer will be less bothered about how far or close their bank is to where they live,' says Addae.

He adds, 'Also, instead of running after every type of customer, can we identify the various customer segments, their current sizes and the future projections for each segment? Imagine that our bank is a human being. Let's figure out what qualities it should have for it to endear itself to a given customer segment. This will help us identify the customer segments we specifically want to cater to, what messages would appeal to them and how we can convey our messages to them at a low cost. Without carrying out this exercise, we'd be wasting our money targeting all kinds of customers and saying what we want, not what they want to hear, resulting in suboptimal outcomes.'

The VP doesn't sound very happy with the way this conversation is going. He mentions that he has received some unique creative ideas from their advertising agency for a TV campaign and that he has already asked them to start a conversation with the agents of some of the biggest football stars.

Addae hears him out patiently and then says, 'We'll do all that when the time comes. But for now, instead of spending a lot of money to get some footballer who has nothing to do with the bank to endorse us, why don't we use our own satisfied customers as brand ambassadors? Yes? And also, please make sure that the customer segment survey I had suggested earlier is conducted properly. I am sure your research agency can help you with that. Once we have the results, let's meet again in my office to take this discussion further.'

That evening Kobby again asks Ekow to accompany him for a walk after dinner. He begins the conversation by enquiring after Ekow's friends from college.

'What's Kojo up to these days?' asks Kobby.

'I don't know. I don't see much of him these days.'

'Why? I thought he was a great friend of yours. Did you guys have a fight?'

'No, we didn't. He just annoys me now and I'm not fond of him anymore.'

'Is it something he said or did that upset you? What did he do to annoy you so much?'

'He didn't do anything to me. It's just that he spends a lot of money, much beyond his means, and is not at all serious about his studies.'

'Did he borrow money from you and didn't return it or has he ever failed his exams?'

'No, neither. But he keeps talking about going for movies and expensive dinners all the time. I don't think he spends any time on his studies. In fact, I don't think he'll do well at college.'

'And what about your other friend, Jose? How's he doing?' asks Kobby.

'Jose is doing well. He's a nice guy. In fact, I'm thinking of asking him to join me as a partner if I ever start that grocery store on the main street.'

'Oh, that's a good idea. What makes Jose so nice?'

'He asks after you guys every time we meet. Also, when Kojo's sister wanted some books that she wasn't getting here, Jose asked his cousin, who was coming from London, to bring them for her. He's always very helpful. I like him a lot.'

'That's very sweet of him. But do you realise what you did just now? You said Kojo is annoying and someone you don't want to meet only because you believe he spends too much money and doesn't do justice to his studies. And you feel this way even though he has never borrowed money from you nor ever failed an exam.'

'Yes. So what?'

'You also said you think Jose is a nice guy and you like him because he is always very polite and because he helped Kojo's sister get a book she wanted.'

'That's true.'

'That means for people to be your friends, you expect them to live up to the values that are important to you. So, they need to be diligent, polite and helpful and not be too extravagant, if they are to be your friends.'

'Maybe,' says Ekow.

'The way you think about them is not based on their behaviour towards you. It is based on what you think they are doing. And if you don't like what someone is doing, you don't even want to meet them.'

'I have never thought of it this way, but you may be right.'

'Customers are also like that. They have expectations from brands they buy from, just like we have expectations from other people. If a brand lives up to those expectations, customers have a good opinion of it and continue to patronise it. But if it doesn't, then customers stop engaging with such a brand. What's more, most of these opinions are based on what they imagine the brands are doing based on its market image, the advertising it does, and other people's experiences and opinions of it. A lot of times customers form their opinions even before they've had any personal experience with the brand.'

'Hmm ...'

'Hence any business should first try to understand the expectations that its customers have from it and build its brand accordingly. And then, the message it sends out to their customers through advertising or other means should be such that it conveys to them that the brand's values match their own.'

'Dad, where did you learn all this from? Are you taking classes in your free time?'

Kobby chuckles and says, 'I have my sources, son. Now go figure out what the customers of a grocer expect from him and see how you can build a brand for yourself that matches their expectations. The day you are ready with all that, we will invest in a store on the main street.'

Ekow looks at Kobby, smiles and they continue to walk. It seems to Kobby that his son has accepted the argument he was making.

A week later, the bank's VP of marketing is again at Addae's office to continue their earlier discussion. He tells Addae that after studying the demographics of banking customers, his team has concluded that even though it is customers who are older who visit the bank most often, their share of deposits has been dropping steadily. On the other hand, the customers in the age group of 30–50 years whose share of deposits is rising the fastest want to avoid visiting the bank as much as possible.

The VP also mentions that he has personally met some customers who belong to both segments and he has observed that the reason customers of an older age don't mind visiting the bank is because they have more time on their hands. They also like to step out of their house more often to carry out chores, pay bills, shop for groceries, attend family gatherings, etc. But customers in the age group of 30–50 years are actually struggling to balance their work and family schedules. Because of a lack of free time, they are increasingly relying on apps that help them carry out their chores digitally from remote locations. To them, going to the bank is another chore they don't have time for, and they would prefer if they could access banking services sitting at home. A lot of YGB's customers in this category also complained to the VP that they aren't happy with the online services provided by YGB. 'Every time we face a problem, the bank insists that we visit the nearest branch for a resolution. We have a life outside of the bank's branch too, you know?' one customer said.

Addae suggests to the VP of marketing that they call a joint meeting with the VP of operations and share these findings with him. Later, when all three of them sit together analysing the results of the customer segment survey, they conclude that the preferred customer segment for YGB are those in the age group of 30–50 years, as they are economically active and digitally savvy. They are more attractive to YGB not only because they bring in more deposits but also since they prefer transacting online instead of visiting a bank physically. So YGB need not spend huge sums in opening more branches. This makes them a more profitable segment.

Addae also feels that if there are customers who choose a particular bank only because of its proximity to where they live, then such customers can easily be serviced by providing them with internet or phone banking services, obviating the need for them to ever visit their bank personally. As per Addae, 'Net banking can help you do everything from your phone' is what YGB should aim for as its key differentiator from its competitors.

The VP of operations promises to work with the IT team to build an app on which a customer will be able to do everything that right now they need to go to a bank for, even something like opening a new account. He asks for six months to complete this task, which Addae is happy to grant. Addae thinks that setting up 200 new branches would have taken much longer and cost the bank much more money than building an app.

The VP of marketing, too, by now, has a clear sense of the brief that he has to pass on to the advertising agency for the marketing campaign. He calls for a meeting with the agency and gives them a list of fourteen actions that the future YGB app will be able to perform and asks them to build a campaign around the app and some of these services. The agency asks for a week to brainstorm and come back with creative ideas.

By now, Kobby and Ekow have gotten into the habit of walking regularly after dinner. They discuss everything under the sun while they walk, from relationships to politics, and sometimes the conversation takes them towards Ekow's business too.

Today, Ekow starts the conversation and Kobby listens to him encouragingly.

'Dad, along with Jose, I visited a few supermarkets to understand what people like most about them.'

'Why supermarkets? I thought you wanted to open a grocery store,' says Kobby.

'What we sell, supermarkets sell too. Jose and I feel that if we can deliver the same services to a customer as a supermarket does, without the customer having to travel all the way to a supermarket, maybe we can build a good grocer brand. Isn't that what you asked us to do?'

'Yes, of course. Good thinking. So, what did you guys find?'

'The first thing that people are seeking is convenience. They like supermarkets because they can find whatever they're looking for in one place.'

'Hmm! But to be able to do that you'll have to have open a very large store, won't you? We don't have that much money,' says Kobby.

'Not necessarily, Dad. Jose suggests that we start with a "Delivery Only" business. We'll open a small store where customers can come and place their orders, or they can place their orders on our website or app. Commercial space is expensive to rent while residential is not. So, instead of keeping our stocks in the store, we'll keep them at home, or rent another house nearby once the business picks up and deliver them directly to the customer's house. This way we'll save the cost of opening and maintaining a large store with a wide variety of stock. More so, we can even consider buying our stocks from the wholesale market based on the orders that have been placed instead of storing things beforehand.'

'But who will build and maintain your store's app and website? It will be expensive. It's easier for large companies to do this, not for shopkeepers,' interrupts Kobby.

'Jose has spoken to his sister, and she can help us set up our website and app.'

'And what about the manpower you'll need to make deliveries at customers' homes? I'm not sure how economically feasible this online model is.'

'Dad, our research has shown us that more and more people are preferring to do their shopping online, including their grocery shopping. They want to sit at home and order whatever they want at the tap of a finger. This online model will make those customers satisfied. As for the manpower needed for deliveries, having a "Deliveries Only" model will save us the cost of hiring salespersons for the grocery store. The cost of deliverymen will be lower than that of salespersons.'

'I can see you've put in a lot of thought into this, Ekow. What else did you find out from your supermarket visits? What else are customers looking for?'

'They are looking for new experiences every time they go shopping. Otherwise it becomes a very boring chore for them.'

'And how do you plan to provide that from a small store?'

'We have decided to have large touch screens in our store instead of physically keeping the stock. Even if customers drop in to our store, we'll make them use the large touchscreens to build their baskets virtually on these screens. Whatever they click on drops into their basket and they can see their basket fill up and the prices add up. At every milestone bill value, a video game will be forwarded to their phone. Kids these days are crazy about video games they can play on their parents' phones. Once the word spreads, their kids will force them to come to our shop and buy from us instead of elsewhere. This will be a unique experience for the customer, as no other store does that so far. It will make the otherwise boring job of buying grocery exciting.'

'What else?'

'Customers are also looking for value for money, which they think supermarkets offer them. So, on these screens we'll also have a comparison of our prices with those offered by prominent supermarkets and e-commerce sites for some frequently shopped products like lentils, oil, soaps, etc. Even if we have to sell some products at cost or even at a loss, we'll more than make up for it on other products if our customers believe that we are not more expensive than the large stores and continue to shop with us.'

'That sounds like a plan, Ekow. I'm sure with some more thinking you'll be able to make it even better. The foundations of your business seem right and I'm happy that Jose is a part of your plan. Not just you, but I, too, have begun to like the boy. Ask him and his sister to join us for dinner someday.'

Next morning, Addae is talking on the phone with his VP of marketing while Kobby drives him to work.

'I saw the ad film scripts your agency sent. I must say I'm a little disappointed. They want us to make five films, one depicting each service that the YGB app will provide, such as opening an account, making a payment, ordering a cheque book, etc., followed by the tagline, "A YGB branch in every phone". Then there is a film that says, "Highest interest rate on your savings, lowest interest rate on your loan".

'I think these scripts are written in the "sell" mode, which almost all advertisers follow, hence they seem commonplace and pedestrian. These kinds of ads seem desperate and don't register with people because they don't establish a connection with them. People like to hear stories that "tell" and not "sell". That tell them how a particular product or service will benefit them, help them grow, become better, etc. Selling is an activity; it can be copied by anyone and you can't own it. In contrast, if you use the medium of telling, you can convey the same benefits by telling an endearing tale that engages them. This tale speaks to a customer's heart, endears your brand to them and this way, as a business, you can own that benefit forever. It becomes yours. Ask the advertising agency to think about the campaign along these lines. Also tell them that iconic brands like Levi's, Nike, Coke, Toyota, etc., did not become what they are by making ads that shouted about their price or product features.'

That evening after dinner, Kobby again brings up the topic of Ekow's store on their walk.

'So have you thought about what you as a grocer would stand for in your customers' minds?' asks Kobby.

'I told you what we are planning Dad. We'll give our customers convenience, excitement and value for money.'

'These are all activities that you will do and soon other stores will start copying you. Once that happens, you'll be lost because they'll be bigger and may have been around for longer.'

'So, what are you suggesting?' asks Ekow.

'I'm not suggesting anything. All I'm saying is that points like convenience, excitement and value for money make for a good sales pitch, but they can easily be copied by others. However, if you talk about how a customer can benefit from using your brand and then back it up on the ground with these activities that you spoke to me about, you will establish an emotional connection with the customer, something which will be difficult for anyone to snatch away.'

'I understand what you are saying, but I'm just a store with a signboard. I'm not a brand that can advertise on TV. So how do I establish an emotional connect?'

'First, TV is not the only way of advertising. In fact, emotional connects are not established only by advertising. Your brand name, your pamphlets, your website and, most important of all, the experience that the customer has while dealing with you will establish that connect. Think about all these things and you will discover many opportunities to build that connect.'

A week later, YGB's agency comes back with just one script for an ad film. It depicts a student preparing for an exam, with different scenes showing him studying in his bed, at his study table, walking in the lawns and other places in the house. In every situation, his mother can be seen in the background preparing a meal or a snack for him, ironing his clothes, heating water for his bath, etc. She is always around him, without ever coming into his line of sight, doing everything she can to help him, without disturbing him one bit. The final voiceover says, 'YGB, silently working behind the scenes, so you can move ahead'. In the final shot, all services a YGB customer will be able to carry out online without visiting a branch are listed.

The VP of marketing sets up a viewing of the film for Addae, who first gets up from his chair and claps, then goes around the room to pat the VP on his shoulder.

'Finally, we have a good property in this mother and child to speak with our customers. If I were you, I'd now identify four or five benefits that customers are seeking from their bank and make sure we mount advertising campaigns round the year to talk about each of these benefits at least once a year. And I'd use the mother and child every time to convey these benefits,' said Addae.

The VP of marketing beams as he diligently notes down Addae's advice.

Addae asks, 'How many people do you have in your team?'

The VP says, 'Not many. Though we have a sanctioned strength of four, we've been able to fill only two positions so far.'

Addae continues, 'While we have landed a great property,

its effective deployment will need trained hands to make the most of it. We'll need to check customer response after every campaign to decide what to say in our next campaign and how. Our media spends will be high, and to buy media efficiently, we may need to hire someone with media sales experience. And there will come a time when this property stops working. We need to know when it does and create another equally endearing property to take over from where this one left off. The game has begun, and we can't drop the ball once it's been lifted. Let us speak with a consultant who'll guide us about an ideal team structure to deliver our ambitions.'

That night Ekow tells Kobby that they have decided to call their grocery store 'You Shop, We Carry' and they will have a slogan which says, 'We want you to spend your time with your family, not with us.' He also mentions that Jose and he are also working on some endearing ways of managing their interactions with customers to reinforce this. 'For instance, we'll have promoters with large backpacks driving around the neighbourhood on branded scooters. While this will reinforce the "You Shop, We Carry" branding, it will also help create an impression that many people are shopping with us, hence we must be a good place to shop.'

Here are some statements that you should respond to for the business that you are a part of, as an owner or a manager. Remember to respond honestly.

The statements must be answered in a yes/no format. If there are any statements that are not relevant to your business, put a cross against them.

- ☐ We understand the core and peripheral benefits that our target customers desire from our product or service.
- ☐ This understanding is formally shared with employees CEO+2 levels and above.
- ☐ All customer propositions and customer touchpoint processes are designed to fulfil these desired benefits.
- ☐ We have an ongoing communication calendar, updated for the next twelve months, to help us deliver the message of our core benefits, at least twice a year.
- ☐ Our advertising focuses on the core benefit while subtly weaving product benefits into the narrative. Specific pricing, markdown and other tactical communication are limited to below-the-line communication.
- ☐ We track brand recall, relevance and intention to purchase for each of the targeted segments, every month.
- ☐ Approval of commercial, service and IT functions is sought before making any change in product propositions and processes.
- ☐ Our customer research and media buying teams are headed by people with prior research agency and media buying experience.
- ☐ The last time our brand recall dipped for a target

segment, it took less than three months to begin recovery.

- ☐ We are the most endearing brand amongst all our competitors.

Now consider the statements to which you have responded with a 'No'. Discuss and reflect on these within your company, read more about **brand management** and/or ask some experts about how to apply these statements to your specific case.

Doing this could help you build a brand which has lasting emotional connect with your customers and stakeholders.

7

A HOUSE FOR EVERYONE

Growing the industry and your share of it

Naqqash picks up his pen, tucks it in the upper pocket of his jacket, rises from his seat at the head of the table in the boardroom of Kismat Constructions and continues to talk while walking towards the door.

'… and this is the last time I'm saying that this company would've been ten times its value, if and only if people had heard my pleas to set its targets with care. Neither too low, nor too high. You know what is more frustrating than people who are unaware? It is people who think that others are more unaware than them. I refuse to preside over a group of people that doesn't know anything and doesn't want to listen to anything either. I am out of here. Call me when you've got your act together.'

With that he walks out and slams the door shut behind

him while Ali and Fazal look at each other with a look that says, 'How do we handle the situation now?'

Kifat was a small-time building contractor in Sargodha, a mid-sized city in Pakistan. He married his uncle's daughter, Ismat, and moved to Lahore, the capital of the Punjab province. Ismat's father was a landlord who hailed from Mustafa Abad, a village 20 kilometres outside Lahore, where the family owned 2,000 acres of land. Ismat being his only child, it was her father's desire to have her husband move in with them and take over the reins of the family business. That's how Kismat Constructions came into being after Kifat and Ismat's wedding.

One of Kifat's early attempts at growing the business after moving to Lahore was the construction of a small residential colony in Mustafa Abad. He cut a small portion of the family land into smaller plots to build the colony. The fact that the land was inherited and not bought at market value, coupled with Kifat's experience of managing construction at a very low cost, combined to result in a good profit for Kismat Constructions. However, because of the colony's distance from Lahore and the lack of proper schooling, shopping and medical facilities, the response to the project was largely from financial investors who were looking for a return on their investment and not serious buyers who wanted to live there. The residential colony remained unoccupied for many years, and Kifat's dream of building more residential colonies around the original one never came to fruition. The original project itself did not give the investors a great return so there was no question of investing any more money in Mustafa Abad.

A couple of years later, Kifat passed away in a road accident, leaving Ismat with the sole responsibility of raising their twin boys, Ali and Fazal. It wasn't as if Kifat had left Ismat in dire straits. He had tended to Ismat's father's estate very well, and rents from the farmers in that area were good enough to support their lavish lifestyle. Kifat also invested the proceeds of his maiden venture in a London bank, which continued to yield handsome returns while Pakistan's continued exchange rate deterioration ensured that their wealth grew, year on year.

In the years that the boys were growing up, Ismat often consulted her uncle Naqqash, who owned a couple of sugar mills near Kot Lakhpat in Lahore. Naqqash was a good sounding board when it came to questions about what and where the boys should study so that, one day, they could handle the construction business and grow the family's wealth.

Both boys went to America for their graduation and, on Naqqash's suggestion, followed it up with postgraduate degrees. While Ali specialised in civil engineering, Fazal was a keen student of finance. The brothers did well in academics, and on their return to Pakistan, they were appointed to the board of Kismat Constructions. Naqqash was made the chairman of the board to make sure the boys continued to have his guidance and the benefit of his experience.

In the years since Kifat built the residential colony in Mustafa Abad, Lahore has expanded in all directions. Many neighbouring villages are included in what is now known as Greater Lahore. The first task that Naqqash sets for Ali and Fazal is to explore growth opportunities in Mustafa Abad so that the family's large land holdings in that area can be put to good commercial use.

Ali and Fazal work hard at this task. From published data, they obtain information about the population and migration numbers of people who moved from other parts of Pakistan to Lahore over the years. They also conduct a survey of other Pakistani cities whose outskirts have already been developed into residential and commercial areas to figure out the rates at which properties were sold there and the kind of facilities these places are providing to the buyers. Some of this data is available in the public domain, but for the rest they meet local brokers and scan through classified ads in newspapers for rent and sale of properties.

They toss around ideas of building a residential colony, a commercial complex or an industrial estate. Eventually, they come up with a five-year plan to convert half of their ancestral land into a township which will have homes of three different sizes, schools, a mall, a hospital and a community centre. They decide to raise funds for the construction of the township partially through advances received from potential buyers and partially from bank loans, whose repayment schedule is factored into the plan.

The plan will utilise 1,000 acres of the total land in Mustafa Abad that the family owns, but the brothers don't plan to sell all the property they construct. They intend to lease a part of it through a leasing division of their own company. The projected return as per their plan is in excess of what needs to be repaid to the banks, hence there is the possibility of earning a good profit from the sale of the properties in the township. Naqqash approves the plan in a long offsite board meeting of the company spanning two days. His closing remarks are: 'Even though this sounds like a good kick-off plan, things might not go exactly as you've planned. You may need to adapt to the situation with every unfolding reality. Also, for executing a plan of this size, you'll need to hire experienced people. Let us build a schedule for the entire project and monitor its progress once every fortnight.'

Ali and Fazal are highly enthused by the plan they have put together and also by Naqqash's words of approval. They get to work the very next morning to start executing the project. For some time, things go as planned. The brothers reach out to some of their erstwhile friends from college and hire them in various roles for the execution of the project. They also engage two American firms to help them with the design and project management aspects of the construction.

It's on the eve of the release of their newspaper advertisement asking for bookings in the township that the unexpected happens. Another builder has taken out a full-page ad in the newspaper, announcing a township similar to theirs in Pandoke, just 12 kilometres away from their site. The prices they have announced are 30 per cent lower than what Ali and Fazal were planning to offer. The ad also announces that the delivery of the project will be done within a year.

At this news, Ali and Fazal feel as if their world has come crashing down around them. Despondent, they visit Naqqash at his home to figure out how they should proceed. Naqqash is smiling as they enter his large living room. He asks the boys to sit and offers them tea and snacks before he starts talking. He doesn't seem too surprised or flustered by what has happened, and says, 'Boys, it's very simple. If their input costs can deliver the project at this price, then so can yours. And if yours can't, then theirs can't either. So go back, rework your costs, negotiate however much you can with your suppliers and figure out from where this other company is sourcing its raw material. And please hire some Pakistanis in your purchase department who are clued in to the local market and have a personal rapport with the suppliers. These suited, booted English-speaking friends of yours won't be able to strike the right deals here. They weren't even able to tell you beforehand that someone was launching a project similar to yours, at a price 30 per cent lower than yours, and just 12 kilometres away from you.'

The boys go back to the drawing board and rework the price of every single line item in the plan, yet they find that there is only a 10 per cent scope for reducing costs. They call for a board meeting to discuss this outcome, to tell the board that they won't be able to reduce the cost of the project to match that of their competitor's. This is when Naqqash loses his cool and storms out of the board meeting. The main reason he is upset is because the new costings that Ali and Fazal have presented to the board have been prepared by the same America-returned purchase managers who made the original plans. The brothers have not heeded Naqqash's advice to hire local, street-smart Pakistani purchase managers to support them.

The evening of the stormy board meeting, Ali and Fazal once again land up at Naqqash's home. By now the latter's anger has subsided, and he tries to explain his point to the boys again.

'Is the builder of the Pandoke project offering homes of the same size as ours?' asks Naqqash.

'Yes, he is. His homes also come in the 3BHK and 5BHK formats,' says Ali.

'How many apartments is he offering vis-à-vis ours?' asks Naqqash.

'He's got plans to release 2,000 apartments while we are building 1,000 apartments.'

'Maybe because his orders with the raw material are larger, suppliers are giving him raw material at lower prices. Did you factor that into your new calculations?' asks Naqqash.

'Yes, we did. That's why we can't match the Pandoke builder's prices,' replies Fazal.

'But what if we changed our plans and increased the number of apartments we are offering to 2,000, even 3,000? Do you think we would get better deals from suppliers if we did that?' Naqqash continues questioning the boys.

'Is there be such a large demand for homes around Lahore? As per our survey, in the last three years, people have bought less than 1,000 homes per year in that area,' says Ali, looking worried.

'If we let only history determine our future, mankind wouldn't make any progress. Now is the time we need to create demand rather than just cater to it. To make our township economically feasible and to be able to compete with other builders, we will have to grow the demand for housing in that area faster than how it would grow organically. And if we are the ones driving this growth, we might even get a larger share of this business than the others. So go and talk to your friends in other industries, if you have any who are working in Pakistan'—he winks as he says this—'and ask them how they go about increasing demand in their respective businesses.'

Ali and Fazal make a list of their friends from school who now work with large international and national companies operating in Pakistan. They can identify four friends who have the kind of experience they are looking for and invite them over for dinner individually in the coming week.

The week of the dinners brings back many memories for the brothers. They exchange anecdotes with their friends about teachers who had strange accents or habits, classmates who would play pranks, accidents in the chemistry lab, trips to Murree and Karachi and many other fun times they had in school. But it is not all fun and games; the brothers know that the task assigned to them by their uncle is very important.

While talking to their friends, Ali and Fazal discover that all international companies that their friends are employed with work with the knowledge that their success depends on growing the market they cater to, because merely servicing the existing demand is not very profitable. The way these companies go about doing this is by enticing people who are currently not their customers into buying their products. They top it up by making current consumers consume even more. The brothers are told by their friends that in most companies, any business plan presentation that the local team makes to the global team has a section that deals with targeted investments, costs and revenue streams from 'industry growth'.

Amir, the friend who works for a personal products company, tells them that a year ago, their sales team informed the strategy team that in the case of cities, there was almost 100 per cent market penetration for products like shampoos, soaps, deodorants, etc., because of which sales were stagnating. To counter the dip in sales, the strategy team came up with the idea of launching their products in smaller sizes, which could be sold at a lower price, thus opening up new markets for the company in city slums and in villages. Given that a greater section of the population fell in the middle and lower-middle class segments as compared to the high-income upper and upper-middle class segments, the company's sales numbers shot up seven times in three years.

Other friends who belong to the packaged foods, two-wheeler and electronic industries have similar stories to tell. In the last few years, they have had to either create a lower-priced version of their existing product with fewer features or launch more variants in the same product category.

Javed, another of their friends, brings an interesting perspective to the discussion, as he suggests something contrarian. He says the increase in the sale of any branded product is not because companies have managed to discover new markets that didn't exist earlier. Since the capacity of human beings to eat, drink, wash or consume any product is finite, brands are not really able to make people consume more than what they used to. It's just that earlier people were consuming unbranded products or products that were being sold loose, and now they are shifting to branded packaged products. Therefore, demand is not being created; rather, unbranded demand is being converted into branded demand. As per Javed, any company that is looking for growth needs to identify people who are already consuming some form of the product, and then find a way to steer their consumption to their own products and brands. Making people consume or do things that they aren't already consuming or doing is a very tough ask.

Once all the dinners are over, the brothers sit down to compare notes.

'There is one common point that almost everyone made

and that is if you want to grow the market, look for new customer segments, preferably from lower-income groups. What did you think of that?' asks Ali.

'That might work in the case of food products and detergents, but how will it work for our industry? I think we just wasted a week talking to our friends without gaining any valuable insights. Though it was fun catching up with everyone after such a long time,' says Fazal.

'I don't agree with that. If selling a smaller size of a product at a lower price opens up a potentially larger customer base, then why wouldn't the same happen in the case of housing? After all, houses are bought by the same people who eat biscuits, drink cola and wash clothes, aren't they?'

'Oh, give me a break, Ali! How can you even compare something that comes out of a packet with something that we live in? The economics of the two businesses are totally different. Remember, I told you to take a couple of more finance courses in college, but you didn't listen and now I must suffer because of your ignorance,' jokes Fazal.

'Just humour me for a while. What if we follow the same model and offer smaller homes that appeal to the masses. One-room, maybe two-room homes?'

'Are you silly or are you silly, Ali? Have you heard of any builder selling one-room homes? One-room homes are most common in ghettos, slums and illegal colonies. People living in these areas prefer to construct their homes themselves, buying bricks, cement and steel on their own because they think that works out to be cheaper. They often don't even plaster the exteriors of their houses because they believe it does not add any structural value to the building other than making it look good, which is something they don't care much about. Drive through Shahdara someday, and you'll be able to see this for yourself. I don't think they would be willing to pay a higher price for the kind of amenities we intend our housing projects to provide, leave alone for the construction quality. Moreover, a lot of them live in rented homes because they don't have enough money left over to build a house after meeting their daily needs, and their poor credit profile doesn't allow them to secure a loan from the bank. I highly doubt there will be any demand for our one-bedroom homes. Where will our target consumers for such dwellings get the money from?'

'What if we offered to sell them the homes on a monthly instalment basis, where the instalments will almost be equal to the rent they currently pay?' asks Ali.

'I wasn't aware that Abba left us a bank along with the estate. Did he? Why didn't anyone tell me about it?'

'Fazal, come on. This is not a joke. I think if we go to the bank and show them that it is to the bank's benefit to finance the purchase of small homes, they might agree to grant such loans. After all, there are bigger margins on small ticket loans.'

'But will they also be willing to take the risk of losing money in case of delinquencies in loan repayment, a prospect that is higher for people with limited means of income?'

'That's the bank's outlook, and they have to find a way around the problem. Ours is only to create a new opportunity that will grow the industry and give us a larger share of the market because we have pioneered the growth.'

'If you're convinced of this plan, then go do the maths, but keep me out of it. With great difficulty, we've got Naqqash uncle back on the discussion table. I don't want to do anything that will annoy him again. Mom won't ever talk to us if she got to know that he's walked out of a board meeting, that too twice.'

The next day, Ali tries to pull up some income and population data pertaining to Lahore. Though some of it is easy to find, most of it isn't. He engages a small-time research firm to go to every low-income residential area in Lahore and its surrounding suburbs, speak to a handful of people residing in each area and figure out whether they own or rent their home, how much rent they pay each month and how much money they are willing to spend to buy a home of their own.

The data takes three weeks to collate. When Ali sees the final presentation deck made by the agency, he can't wait to break the news to Fazal because the numbers are mindboggling.

According to the data, there are forty times more one- and two-room homes in certain areas of Lahore than there are homes with three or more rooms. Rough back-of-the-envelope calculations show that on account of economies of scale, if Kismat Constructions builds these small homes, the cost incurred by them will be lower than the cost incurred by people who build their own homes. Ali decides that this can be the USP of the small homes—that they are homes of good quality built by a well-known builder but they are affordable for the lower-income class. Ali tells Fazal, 'And, if we manage to sell our homes to 10 per cent of the people who are currently renting a small home, we could be selling volumes that would be four to five times of what we had planned earlier.' Fazal still doesn't look convinced, but reluctantly agrees to accompany Ali to a meeting with Naqqash.

Naqqash loves the numbers when he sees them and asks the boys, 'Do you think a person who wants to buy a smaller home at low cost might be more willing to accept lower specs for corridor sizes, amenities, flooring, etc., in the building as opposed to someone who's spending the big bucks to buy a four-room home? I'd say yes.'

'I guess they would,' agrees Ali.

'The scale of this project, if we include the small homes too, will help us negotiate harder with our suppliers and get the best prices in the market for the raw material.'

'I am sure it would,' says Ali.

'We could even talk to the bank into giving a preferential rate, which we could merge into our pricing and offer "interest-free instalments" to small-home buyers. That could be your second proposition to your customers in addition to "pay only what you pay as rent and get your own home".'

'I could even go speak to someone in the government for some subsidies because our project would be providing homes to lower income groups. We have elections next year and I'm sure they are looking for a new plank to please the masses,' agrees Fazal, finally getting on board with the plan.

'Uncle, with all of these events coming together, we could run out of our ancestral 2,000 acres,' says Ali.

'Ha ha, don't worry, we'll just buy more land,' is Naqqash's final word.

Here are some statements that you should respond to for the business that you are a part of, as an owner or a manager. Remember to respond honestly.

The statements must be answered in a yes/no format. If there are any statements that are not relevant to your business, put a cross against them.

- ☐ We use data from published industry sources and projections from adjacent industries to set our targets.
- ☐ Our price and market share assumptions are not linear. They consider potential entry of new competitors, desperate market share gain moves by competitors, industry consolidation possibilities, changes in our portfolio, etc.
- ☐ In the last five years, our industry size projection has not varied by more than 2 per cent from the actual industry size.
- ☐ For years with deviations greater than 2 per cent, we analyse the reasons for the deviations and try to attribute them to specific causes such as data source error, ignored adjacencies, etc.

- ☐ We have made at least one major modification to our industry size projection process in the last one year.
- ☐ In the last two years, every time we have forecast a shortfall against target, we have created an action plan to cover a part of the gap within a month of the reforecast.
- ☐ We have staff dedicated to creating industry projections, benchmarking and performing ongoing reviews.
- ☐ In the last two years, we have not experienced a shortfall of human or capital resources required to implement planned revenue growth initiatives.
- ☐ Our senior commercial teams are rewarded for increasing revenue and margin share, and not just for meeting or beating budgeted sales targets.
- ☐ Our front-line teams have access to near real-time revenue reports for their territories.

Now consider the statements to which you have responded with a 'No'. Discuss and reflect on these within your company, read more about **effective scaling** and/or ask some experts about how to apply these statements to your specific case.

Doing this could help you grow the size of your industry as well as your business many times over.

8

FROM POWERPOINT TO 'ONE-POINT'

Using focused reviews to create and drive agenda

'Can one drive a car while looking in the rear-view mirror? Trust me, Joe, I am driving this bloody company in that mode. And it sucks!'

Saying that, Gavin slams his glass on the bar, signalling to the barman for another double.

Gavin has been at the helm of Trinity—the largest internet service provider in New Zealand—for three months now. Trinity is a pioneer of the industry and was formed in the early 1990s, when internet speeds were still being measured in kilobytes. It had the first pick of the country's premium customers, before its competitors came into the market and started providing customers with relatively cheaper plans. Its network is considered reliable, it is renowned for the quality of its service and, over the years, it has had some of the most admired advertising campaigns across industries.

But the dynamics of the industry have changed over time. Fibre has replaced copper, broadband has replaced dial-up, streaming has replaced buffering and mesh has replaced routers. One after the other, new players have entered the market without any baggage of legacy and invested large sums of money in new technologies. Incumbent players have had to make a great deal of effort to convince their boards that it is in their best interest to dump old infrastructure and replace it with the new. Some players like Trinity have survived this overhaul, while several others have fallen by the wayside.

Trinity is fortunate to have a very engaged board. They understand that running a technology business is like running on a treadmill—if you don't move with the speed of the changing times, you fall off. Gavin deeply understands the nature of the business and stated at a company dinner, a few weeks after joining Trinity: 'I wish my parents and my wife had understood me as well as Trinity's board understands this industry. I'd have been so much farther ahead in life.'

The last three months at Trinity have not really been a great experience for Gavin though. While the business has been doing well and customers have continued to subscribe without any complaint, Gavin isn't happy with what he has seen so far. He spent his initial weeks in meeting various members of the Trinity organisational structure, but they haven't given him the confidence that Trinity will be able to survive if a competitor or a new entrant starts offering a unified data and content plan. It is surprising to Gavin that no one has attempted to do this in New Zealand so far, not even Trinity.

At his very first meeting with the senior leaders' team, or SLT as they are known around the company, he senses some very cold vibes between the team members. It feels as if he is in a dog park where each dog has marked its territory and growls at any other dog that dares to stray into it. And when a growl doesn't seem to be enough to discourage the encroacher, the dog starts barking loudly, making constructive conversation impossible. He has also noticed that there is very little social conversation or friendly banter between the members. Meetings invariably end with everyone just picking up their notepads and walking out—without even exchanging glances, leave alone saying any words—to corners where their respective teams sit.

In these meetings, all Gavin does is watch the endless series of PowerPoint presentations that show how at Trinity the network uptime is being maintained, defects are reducing, recoveries are happening faster, bandwidth costs are dropping and manpower productivity is rising. Invariably, every such review covers a period that spans two to three years because data needs to be plotted over a significant period of time to show any changes.

These details are no different than the information that comes to him every morning in formatted daily reports, and he often finds himself responding to WhatsApp messages, deleting spam mail or even yawning during these meetings. Any suggestion he makes for a change in process is argued against because one or the other team does not consider it to be important or is short of resources to take it on priority. Gavin has started feeling frustrated with his job. He knows that the reason he has been brought to Trinity is to shake things up, and not to sit through boring presentations about what happens each day in every department.

Gavin finally decides that he needs to start throwing his weight around if he wants things to change. Just before the holiday season, Gavin sends out an email saying that a week later he will review each team's readiness for the one and only annual opportunity they have to boost sales—the holiday season at the end of the year. Over the next one week, all teams huddle in their respective corners or in the conference rooms. Any request for a meeting with any of the teams is met with a standard response, 'After the review meeting with the CEO, please.'

Even though Gavin would like to have a joint meeting of all the teams or at least the team heads, each team proposes to meet him separately. They all make presentations loaded with data, graphs and tables. Looking at the volume of the outcome, Gavin knows that hours and hours have gone into creating them.

In their presentation, the sales team gives the sales numbers for the upcoming season based on an analysis of market seasonality in the past four years. The number projected by them is a tad above Gavin's expectations, and it appears they are relying on a higher discount to make these numbers a reality. The commercial team presents three attractive propositions to stimulate customer demand. Gavin is surprised at the team's understanding of customer needs, which has led to the formulation of these propositions. The team in charge of the supply chain informs him that they have already placed orders for routers, fibre, etc., anticipating an increase in demand and have mobilised additional warehousing facilities nearer the markets for speedy service. The team in charge of field service has asked service partners to hire and train more installers for faster installation of customer orders. The marketing team has planned a TV campaign with the advertising agency, specifically focused on the holiday season.

Gavin makes notes during each presentation and presents a summary in the next SLT meeting, saying: 'I met all of you last week and was impressed with what I saw and heard. Very slick and passionate presentations! However, what I noticed was a clear gap in communication between the teams. The projections made by sales team are way more than the procurement, warehousing and carriage arrangements made by the supply chains team. Even if that was something that could be fixed, these sales projections are based on very high discounts. If we take into account the cost we will incur in giving the discounts and the cost of running the advertising campaign the marketing team has planned, it will take us at least ten years to break even on our investment at current prices. We all know that the expected life of a customer in our business is roughly seven years, then how can we ever hope to recover our investment? I am disappointed to see the lack of coordination between the teams. I really wish plans for the holiday season had been made more cohesively, in consultation with each other.'

In the first week of January, SLT meets for the first time since the holiday season. Gavin's predictions have come true. As expected, the projected sales fell short because the supply chain team failed to purchase enough routers in advance to service the demand. This meant that technicians hired from service partners didn't have enough work during the season, but were still paid their full contracted wages at the end of it. Only the marketing team has seen some success—the advertising agency they engaged ran a great campaign for the season, which has been lauded in two marketing journals.

In this meeting, Gavin is wearing a look of deep disappointment and resignation. The debacle of the holiday season planning is preying on his mind. He decides that it is the new year and from now on, he will make sure that things are done differently in the company. He draws the attention of SLT members to the fact that market penetration of internet/

WiFi connectivity is now almost at 100 per cent in New Zealand, and that there are hardly any homes left that don't have WiFi. He says that in order to find new sources of growth, Trinity needs to look beyond broadband. He tells the team that internet service providers in the US have started bundling provisions for security cameras or subscriptions to apps like Netflix, Hulu, etc., along with their WiFi connections to entice more customers, create brand loyalty and grow revenue and margins. Gavin feels this is the way forward for Trinity and asks the team to come up with suggestions, followed by plans that can be implemented.

Gavin knows that initiatives such as this require close coordination between different departments and teams. He hopes that the failure arising from the lack of coordination in planning for the holiday season will have made the teams realise that this time they need to sit together, brainstorm and come up with a joint proposal. But Gavin has hoped in vain. After a fortnight, he is once again made to sit through six different presentations, all of which provide almost identical information on the ways in which operators in other countries are bundling their services.

Gavin is furious because his teams seem to have taken two precious weeks only to come back and give him information that is widely available in the public domain, something he could have found for himself. He thinks, where is the coordination? Where is that well thought-out joint proposal on how Trinity could bundle its services? Why is it that his teams are not paying any attention to what he is saying?

Without saying a word to anyone in the conference room, Gavin storms out.

The next morning, he wakes up to a few missed calls, many messages and more than hundred tweets, all complaining that the Trinity network has been down since last night. People are more angry than usual because last night the final match of that year's English Premier League Championship was being broadcast, but people were unable to watch it because Trinity's network was down. He is also getting reports of a mass exodus of Trinity customers to other internet service providers in the wake of the network failure.

Gavin calls for an emergency session of the SLT to get to the root of the problem. The head of operations says it is an IT failure, but the IT department blames it on a usage surge during the game, which created a load on the network and caused it to trip. Both of them blame the marketing team, who apparently forced them to set very high data caps, which meant that the network speed for customers exceeding their data limits never automatically reduced. Marketing says that they have been asking the sales team to introduce tiered pricing plans for a long time. If that happened, there would be fixed data limits for each plan and the problem that arose last night would not have arisen. This would have also helped in higher revenue generation, which would have provided the necessary finances for the operations and IT teams to enhance network capacity. But, apparently, sales refused to introduce tiered plans until the competition changed their plans too. All that sales had to say was, 'Network management is not our job.'

That evening, while he is at Auckland airport for his flight, Gavin runs into an old friend, Joe. They decide to head to the airport bar to get a couple of drinks. Gavin and Joe worked together over a decade ago and were now in similar roles at different companies, Gavin in telecom and Joe in FMCG. That day, Gavin is so frustrated that while talking he blurts out that running his company is like driving a car while looking in the rear-view mirror.

After sympathetically listening to Gavin's despair, Joe's parting words to Gavin are, 'Your review meeting seems to be stuck on what didn't work and who's to blame for it, while the rest of the world has started using these meetings to set the agenda for the future and to align teams to it. You need to do something similar in Trinity meetings.'

Something that Joe said stays with Gavin during his flight to Christchurch, and he makes copious notes on how Trinity meetings can change. On landing, he messages his assistant, asking her to block the entire morning next Monday for an SLT meeting.

On Monday, Gavin opens the meeting by asking each department head to come up to the white board and write down the key metrics they measure frequently to figure out if their department's performance is on track. Once everyone is done, there are over a hundred items listed haphazardly on the whiteboard.

Gavin then asks the CFO if he can work with the IT department to create a dedicated team of people who will pull, collate and update all this data in one Excel spreadsheet. The CFO and IT heads look at each other dubiously, and the CFO hesitantly says, 'This would take a couple of weeks, but it is possible to create and maintain a central repository of all these reports in one place. But I wonder why we are doing all this. After all, we are tracking all of these metrics in any case.'

Gavin smiles and announces, 'From today onwards, PowerPoint presentations are banned in Trinity, and so are separate department review meetings. There will be a common review every month, attended by every member of the SLT. However, no one need prepare any presentation for this monthly meeting, as data for your department's parameters will be collected and maintained on a spreadsheet by the team appointed by the CFO and supported by the IT department. We will together look at the facts on the screen, look at trends for opportunities or threats and only debate those solutions that can potentially help change the direction or at least the slope of the trend. If any department foresees any problem in implementing the solution that is being discussed in this meeting, they will have to speak up during the meeting itself so that we can think of an alternative or consider the time or cost implications of overcoming the hurdle. I'd also like to give a catchy name to this monthly meeting. Any suggestions?'

No one says a word. Everyone in the conference room is sitting quietly as if trying to digest what just happened. Gavin's assistant, who is there to take notes of the meeting, speaks up, 'Since the meeting will discuss facts as presented by only one data source, how about calling it "the one-point meeting". It will also remind us not to use PowerPoint to prepare for the meeting.'

Gavin smiles at the suggestion and everyone else nods in assent.

Russel, a young management information system (MIS) executive, is assigned by the CFO to collate and update the one-point data. It is not the easiest job because he can't get any of the teams to agree on what the format for the data spreadsheet should be. Most teams are hesitant to put forth any data that shows them in a negative light, even if the data that makes them look good isn't very relevant. It is clear that the teams are still competing with each other and haven't really understood the purpose of the one-point meeting. However, Russel is persuasive and manages to extract as much data from the teams as possible.

The CFO takes Russel to Gavin to give him an idea of what he is in for in the first meeting. Gavin is impressed with what Russel has achieved in less than two weeks and reassures him, 'Don't worry. We will extract the remaining information from them during the meeting itself.'

The first one-point meeting is a unique experience for the

older employees of Trinity. Never before, in the two decades of Trinity's existence, has any SLT member presented their department's data in the presence of colleagues who belong to different departments. One person murmurs to his neighbour, 'This reminds me of the first time I stood naked in my school gym's changing room. I guess eventually we'll get used to this, too, just like we got used to that.'

Russel takes the SLT members through the 130 Excel sheets one at a time, while Gavin sits quietly, trying to see a pattern in the data. Now and then, he asks a few questions to the different department heads, such as 'Let's look at the subscriber data. Wellington seems to have more subscribers per square mile than Auckland. Are the incomes in Wellington higher or are plot sizes far smaller, increasing the number of subscribers per square mile?'

'It's difficult to make this out simply by looking at the homes in Wellington from outside. If marketing could help us get hold of region-wise income data, we could check if there is a corelation,' says the sales head.

'If the incomes are actually higher in Wellington, we could experiment with introducing our new plans to provide internet connections bundled with home security software or OTT apps in Wellington first,' says the marketing head.

There are several nods across the room.

'Why are salespeople getting higher productivity in North Island? Are they trained better or are people in North Island more hardworking or are they doing something different?' asks Gavin.

'I am sure it is our people who are working hard,' says the sales head.

'If that is the case, why don't we send some of our salespeople from other regions to North Island towns? They can accompany North Island salespeople on sales calls for a week or so. For the salesmen in North Island, it would be a sign of our appreciation for their hard work, while visiting salesmen can learn new tricks from them and replicate them in their respective markets,' says Gavin.

The sales head looks at the marketing head, and they agree to meet after the meeting to discuss next steps.

'Let's move to field service now. Defects within thirty days of installation or repair are the highest in Hamilton and Wanganui, almost two times that of other regions. Can we figure out the most common reason for the defects and run special trainings for our field technicians?' says Gavin.

'Sure,' agrees the field service head.

'You can ask the HR department for help to organise training camps for your technicians,' suggests Gavin.

The HR head nods at the service head, assuring him of his team's support in running the training camps.

'Let's talk about the tariff plans next. People who are on lower value plans are inactive for five more days every month as compared to the company average because they do not recharge after their balance gets over for a few days. Can we run an upsell programme to move these customers to six-month or annual plans?' asks Gavin, looking at the commercials head.

'Yes, we can. Even at a 10 per cent discount it would be profitable for us. And it'll also save us the cost of making reminder calls and sending messages every month to such consumers.'

'Any reason for a surge in complaint calls in the second week last month?' asks Gavin, turning to the customer operations head.

'A fibre got accidentally cut in the Westport region and took twenty-four hours to fix.'

'Do we not have a disaster recovery backup option in the region?' asks Gavin.

'We thought we did, but it seems both our main provider and our backup provider were leasing the same background network.'

'And we are being charged twice for it? That's preposterous. Let's talk to them and make sure at least one of them moves to a different network. Can we send one of them debit notes for the last year? Also, can we occasionally swap traffic to the disaster backup network, to make sure they remain prepared for any emergency?' says Gavin.

'Sure,' says the network head.

'And do we send a message to the customers of a particular area if the network is down or if we discover a local fault, along with the expected timelines for recovery? At least that would reduce their anxiety and stop them from calling us non-stop, jamming our lines?'

'The network and field service team have to inform us about an outage for us to send such messages,' complains the customer service head.

'Don't they?' asks Gavin.

'We will put a process in place for that soon.'

'I see more call surge occasions in the previous two months than in the six months prior. Any reasons?' asks Gavin.

'There was a planned CRM upgrade that started two months ago and lasted for six weeks. Maybe it was because of that,' replies the network head.

'Is every service outage discussed between the IT department and the network department? We need to find the root cause of the outage, agree on it, solve the issue with a hardware, software or a process change so that we don't have another outage for the same reason again. I hope you all understand that. I don't mind us failing, but failing for the same reason? No! Unacceptable!' says Gavin forcefully.

'We at customer operations would also like to have a say in this exercise. After all, we are the ones who suffer the most when one or both of you guys make a mistake.'

'I agree. Why don't we add another sheet to the one-point meeting database? It will record every service outage, record the reason for it, the way in which the outage was fixed, the date when it was fixed, etc. In the spreadsheet, put this row of data in red or amber until you get a sign-off on this from the network, IT and customer operations heads. After that, you can change the colour to green so that we all know that it is done.'

'Sounds good,' says Russel.

'Also, let us have the next one-point meeting in Christchurch. We could all travel there one day early, have dinner with the local team and run the meeting the next morning,' suggests the sales head.

'That sounds like a great idea,' agrees Gavin.

The meeting goes on for another hour in the same vein, with each team bringing forth their issues and directly speaking to the concerned department regarding the solution. People are exchanging glances and nods, fixing up meetings with each other to take forward what is being discussed. Gavin is all smiles because these were the very same people who before the meeting would not even look each other in the eye.

Once the meeting is over and everyone has walked out in twos and threes, Gavin turns to Russel and gives him a nod of appreciation.

A month later, Gavin enters the airport bar on his way to Christchurch for the next one-point meeting. He notices Joe sitting on a bar stool.

'Hey, Joe, do you live here? I see you here every time I'm at the airport,' jokes Gavin.

'I could say the same for you, Gavin.'

With that Gavin points towards the bartender and says: 'Bring us two doubles of the most expensive malt you have in the house, repeat them after ten minutes, and bring the bill to me please. My friend here deserves all the thanks I can give him.'

Here are some statements that you should respond to for the business that you are a part of, as an owner or a manager. Remember to respond honestly.

The statements must be answered in a yes/no format. If there are any statements that are not relevant to your business, put a cross against them.

- ☐ All products and services that contribute to more than 3 per cent of our organization's revenue are reviewed monthly to check for market penetration, usage per user and unit price realisation.
- ☐ Our current annual plan has identified at least two programmes with committed resources to drive industry growth.
- ☐ Our review meetings track the movement of our market share individually for every geography that contributes 2 per cent of total revenue.
- ☐ We have launched special plans to stimulate underperforming geographies, with inputs in areas like distribution, visibility, competitive customer offering, etc.
- ☐ Our best salespeople are allocated to underperforming geographies.
- ☐ We have a timebound 'stimulate or abandon' plan for underperforming products and programmes which is reviewed monthly.
- ☐ We have action plans to reduce costs that contribute to more than 1 per cent of our revenue and are rising, which are reviewed every month.

- ☐ Critical customer experience parameters have been identified, failures recorded, root cause analysis carried out and a permanent solution to eliminate cause is implemented. This is captured on a heat map that uses green, amber and red colours to highlight the severity of the issues and the state of closure of every issue.
- ☐ Every action point identified during reviews leads to a project. Projects are managed by teams comprising representatives from at least three functions. Progress and closure of projects are tracked by the project management team.
- ☐ We spend more time reviewing and acting on outcomes of review meetings as compared to preparing for the review meetings.

Now consider the statements to which you have responded with a 'No'. Discuss and reflect on these within your company, read more about **collaborative culture** and/or ask some experts about how to apply these statements to your specific case.

Doing this could help you run your review meetings in a manner that allows you to set your organisation's agenda instead of only discovering what and who is not working.

9

A HEALTHY TEAM ENGAGES EVERYONE

Creating a productive work culture

Dinaz Khorsandi is sitting at one end of a large meeting room in the head office of WeSolve located in Shoreditch, an upcoming and hip business district in East London. She sips her coffee while Paul, the outgoing CEO, takes her through his handover presentation.

In 1979, an eight-year-old Dinaz migrated with her family from Iran to settle in Manchester. After doing a few odd jobs, her father started a grocery store in their neighbourhood. Dinaz continued to live with her family till she finished school. She later moved to London for higher education and found a job in the city after completing her post-graduation. Four jobs, three cities and twenty-five years later, she is here at WeSolve as its new CEO.

WeSolve is in the highly sought-after B2B fintech space. It provides plug-and-play solutions to small and medium enterprises, helping them to focus on their craft without having to bother about any of the supporting services needed to run their business—services in which they have limited or no expertise. The company started as a white-label billing and accounting firm, but later added multiple layers to their services, including desktop publishing, tax calculation and submission, housekeeping, etc., to name a few.

Today Paul is talking to Dinaz about the people and culture of WeSolve. 'Our culture here is made up of two key elements. One, "we do not take what is not ours" and second, "we give back to the community we are doing business with". Each of our employees has adopted either a school, a toilet complex, a public garden or something similar near their homes, and they devote at least four working hours a week towards its upkeep and maintenance. WeSolve helps them financially if the adopted facility does not have access to resources. It makes everyone of us feel so proud and it binds us together too.'

'And how does this help build WeSolve's work culture or deliver its business objectives?' asks Dinaz.

'It makes our employees humbler and more considerate towards society in general, which reflects in their behaviour towards their colleagues and towards our customers.'

'I agree. These are behaviours our parents inculcated in us, and well-run companies should encourage and reward them.'

'This work culture makes our people stand out in a world full of fly-by-night operators. It also helps our people get a foot in the door with potential customers.'

'And how are our people attrition levels?' asks Dinaz.

'Fintech is a tough space to be in these days. People with experience are in short supply, and most companies in our space are well funded, so there is a lot of poaching of good people going on. Our attrition levels are no different from that of others in our industry.'

'And has the productivity of our people been growing?'

'As I said, we are in a very competitive space. Maintaining our productivity itself is an achievement.'

'Can you ask ten or twelve of our people to come in right now? Anyone will do, any function or level.'

'Why?'

'It won't take long. Just for ten minutes.'

Paul asks his assistant to get ten or twelve people to the conference room.

'Hello, everyone! Meet your new CEO, Dinaz. She has something to say to you,' says Paul as soon as everybody enters.

'I just wanted to ask you something. Can each of you tell me one word that according to you describes the work culture at WeSolve?'

'Trust.'

'Pride.'

'People first.'

'Freedom of expression.'

'Consensus-driven.'

'Care and concern.'

'Family.'

'Integrity.'

Answers fly in from all corners of the room. Dinaz diligently notes down all the words in a small notepad she takes out from her handbag.

'Thank you. And I am looking forward to meeting with all of you in the coming days,' says Dinaz.

That evening, on her way home, Dinaz takes out her notebook and starts to ponder over the 'work culture' words that her team came up with.

Dinaz has always believed that culture is a set of shared attitudes, values, goals and practices that differentiate an organisation. The list of words staring at her are largely values. While she strongly believes that values are a core and non-negotiable part of a culture, it takes more than just values to create a work culture that propels and sustains growth. Values alone can create a happy club, not some place that delivers results.

Within a week of joining, Dinaz decides to go around to all areas within the UK where WeSolve provides its services, meeting employees and customers. Over the next two weeks, she meets barbers, coffee shop owners, fabricators, boating club operators, a homeowner who leases eight Airbnb apartments out in Glasgow and Edinburgh and many other customers like these who have accidently become businessmen while following their passion. They all turned to WeSolve to avoid getting weighed down by the procedures and complexities that come with running a business.

Chatting with customers, she hears some positive things about WeSolve:

'I like the way I can just punch in my sale transactions all day and, at the end of the day, I get a summary of what I've sold, how much I've earned and what I need to purchase to replenish my stock,' says one customer.

'When my desktop isn't able to help me, I call the WeSolve helpline, and they give me a solution without making me wait,' says the coffee shop owner using WeSolve services.

There are a few complaints and lots of feedback too.

'WeSolve's database of the local housekeeping services is often not updated. I have to call at least three plumbers before I find one who is still a plumber. People change jobs, but WeSolve's database doesn't seem to know that. It should,' says one grumpy customer.

'WeSolve is great when it comes to managing my billing. But for tax purposes I still go to my local consultant because I am not convinced that people in WeSolve understand Welsh laws,' says a barber in Wales.

'WeSolve helps me manage my business. I wish they could also help me with finding leads to grow my business,' says the Airbnb homeowner.

'We normally wait for anything new from WeSolve to stabilise before we subscribe to it. The first edition is invariably full of bugs.'

'WeSolve may not be the most efficient but for all its flaws, it is an honest company and we trust it.'

On the other hand, WeSolve employees tell her: 'Different

departments at the head office often send conflicting circulars to us and that complicates our life. I wish they spoke amongst themselves first before issuing circulars.'

'Can we test our new services with smaller groups before formally launching them? Frequent failures and buggy software don't help build the confidence of our customers in WeSolve.'

'We are almost never the first ones to come out with a new service. Our competitors beat us to it every time.'

'Though we have regular appraisals every year, the increase in remuneration is not proportionate to our performance. It seems the company doesn't believe in recognising and rewarding people and seems to treat everyone the same, irrespective of how much hard work they put in.'

'My manager got angry with me because I spoke to the service team at the head office directly instead of going through him. But I only did it to save time, then why am I being punished for it?'

'I was transferred from my hometown because I spent a lot of time in trying to land a large local hotel chain as a client, which eventually did not work out. But we did learn from that experience and later managed to land a twenty-outlet restaurant chain as a client.'

'I am not sure what WeSolve expects of me. No one has ever told me and I am expected to depend on the internet to stay abreast of the latest in the industry,' says one of the members of Edinburgh's sales team.

'I was scolded when we did not get an account we were

chasing in Essex. I thought the sales guys were in charge. We were just support,' says a marketing person.

There are many such statements that Dinaz notes in her notepad during the trip. Later she browses through them on her short flight from Edinburgh to London. She decides to bunch most of the statements into three categories.

The first category includes statements which indicated a lack of cohesion and collaboration between the different teams at WeSolve. Both customers and employees complained about faulty, bug-laden new releases. Her experience tells her that the reason for this could be that the teams which are supposed to work together, from ideation to creation, from testing to roll-out, are just not doing that. Dinaz is aware that virtually delivered products require people from at least three or more functions to work together through the different stages of product development and release, so that the product that eventually lands on a customer's desk is without bugs.

The second category has statements that show that experimentation is not being encouraged in the company. WeSolve started as a provider of accounting software for restaurants and later expanded to provide additional services to different kinds of businesses. But has the company fully exploited the idea of providing a bouquet of services to customers and has it reached out to all kinds of businesses? From her conversations, it didn't seem like that. Employees told her about not being rewarded for their innovative ideas or for trying out new things. They also told her about the low tolerance for failure at WeSolve.

The third category that Dinaz identifies comes from statements that indicate there is diffused accountability at WeSolve. Sometimes when she asked, 'Who's in charge?', two or more hands went up in response or none did. It seems to her that WeSolve needs to define new norms for ownership.

Having zeroed in on these three broad themes, Dinaz starts typing out her first communication to all the employees of WeSolve, as the plane starts its descent into London. The solution is so clear in her head that she is done with typing the email by the time the plane lands:

> Dear All,
>
> In the last thirty days that I've been a part of WeSolve, I've met and spoken with many colleagues and customers to learn about the things we do, the things we don't do and the things we could do. I'd like to continue this practice of meeting people regularly. I am aware that like every one of us wants our favourite football club to win, we also want the company to which we give most of our waking hours to win. What does winning mean for WeSolve? To me it means a company with the highest revenue and the highest profit in the fintech sector in the country.
>
> However, we won't become the largest on a wish and a prayer. We could get there by bringing more industries under our fold, followed by making inroads into at least three firms in each industry that we serve.
>
> Problem-solving does not require only investments and people. It requires a unique work culture, our own way of working that makes it easier for us to identify and solve our customers' problems.

My interactions with many of you has helped me zoom in on three unique work behaviours which together add up to the acronym 'CEO'.

Let me start by saying that I am redesignating each of you as CEO from today. No, I'm not kidding and you can let your family know that too. The three alphabets in the CEO designation stand for what each of us needs to strive for, if WeSolve has to win.

The 'C' in CEO stands for collaboration or working together. I have chosen collaboration as our first work behaviour because humans inherently do not like to work in teams. Given a choice, a footballer would prefer to dribble the ball from one end of the field to the other, score a goal, acknowledge the cheers of the spectators, lift the trophy and go home. So we made rules for the game of football that do not allow one person to do everything and, as a result, both the players and the spectators enjoy themselves when eleven players in each of the two teams collaborate for ninety minutes and the team that has highest collaboration between its players wins. Some of you who have had a second child with a gap after the first would have realised how difficult it is for the first child to accept the second in the house. This applies to humans who deliver business results too.

So let us start identifying the other people who can help us deliver our objectives, reach out to them and gain their commitment to help us.

The letter 'E' stands for experimentation. It is what pushed the Wright brothers to fly, so that one day each one of us could fly too. It also led to the invention of the wheel, fire, penicillin, plastics, internet, mobile phone, SMS, email, satellites and so many other amazing things. I could go on and on. All these experiments were conducted decades ago, and their outcomes make our life easier today.

Our customers face problems in multiple areas while running their businesses. Some of these problems may not be related to the services we provide. But still, can we think of solutions to every problem our customers face, allowing them to just stay focused on growing their businesses? And can we put these solutions to work?

It is likely that a lot of times our efforts will not lead us to a product or a solution that we can sell to our customers. Probably more of our attempts will fail than succeed. But if we don't experiment, we'll never know.

The other thing I hear very often is, 'Oh! I tried to do this in 2009 in another company and it didn't work. So now, I won't waste my time trying to do it again.' To me that seems like someone saying, 'I tried to teach our son how to drive when he was ten, and he couldn't learn because his feet didn't reach the ground. So, I'm never going to spend time trying to teach him again.' Folks, your son is eighteen years old now, he has grown taller and now his feet reach the ground. Maybe if you try one more time, this time you will succeed in teaching him how to drive. Don't be afraid to experiment with things that did not work earlier. With modifications and under changed circumstances, they just might work the second time.

Now we come to the letter 'O' in CEO. It stands for ownership.

> When we get down to identifying and solving our customers' problems while collaborating and experimenting, we'll be working in teams.
>
> I want all of you to remember that a team can only have one owner who is in charge, even if there are four to five people assigned to the same task. If there are four people in a car, and it is not a driverless car, the steering wheel can be held by only one pair of hands. Imagine if everyone or no one took charge of steering the car? Would we get anywhere? This applies to our tasks in the company too. And the owner of the task need not be the senior-most person in the team, just as the driver of the car isn't.
>
> Welcome aboard, dear CEOs. Have fun!
>
> Dinaz

She sends this mail to the HR head from the taxi on her way home. She also tells her to ask her team to brainstorm for ideas to publicise and sustain the CEO movement.

In the next Monday meeting, the HR team sounds excited about the initiative, and they have come up with several ideas to give flight to the initiative.

One person suggests they provide each employee with a personalised stationery kit, a mug and a water bottle with their name and the word 'CEO' etched on it. Actually seeing the designation 'CEO' in print under their names would make them believe that what Dinaz has said is not merely talk, but rather something that the company strongly believes in.

Another team member suggests they create a section on WeSolve's intranet and ask people to post stories of successful acts of collaboration, experimentation or ownership around them. From amongst the entries received, a panel can select the most deserving twenty-odd entries every quarter, and the reward for the winners can be a day spent exclusively with Dinaz.

Dinaz laughs at the thought and says, 'Would that be a reward for them or punishment?' However, she loves both the ideas and asks how soon they can arrange for all this. She is in a hurry to kick off the initiative at the next all-hands meeting. The team is confident that it will be able to deliver everything within a week. Their optimism surprises Dinaz, but she starts preparing for the meeting in her head.

On Friday evening, before she leaves office, Dinaz sends out to all WeSolve employees the email she typed on the flight the previous week. She feels that it will give everyone enough food for thought over the weekend to ask questions at next Monday's all-hands meet.

At the all-hands meeting, Dinaz starts by taking everyone through the contents of her mail, which HR has converted into a presentation. By this time, the HR team has delivered the personalised stationery, mugs, etc., to every workstation. Throughout the day, Dinaz has seen smiles all around the office as people opened the wrapping paper. Now she looks at the WeSolve employees and reiterates to them that they are all

CEOs. Then she explains in detail to them the three elements that combine to make up the word CEO—collaboration, experimentation and ownership. She tells them what she expects from them and the need for them to prepare the three sheets she mentioned in her email.

Dinaz notices that even though at the beginning of the meeting people looked uncomfortable interacting with a new leader for the first time, half way through the meeting the tension has eased. People have started lowering their guard and asking questions. In fact, the questions are getting more and more contrarian as the meeting progresses. Dinaz tries to provoke even more discussion by expressing some out-of-the-box thoughts, to which the audience responds with matching candour.

'In uncertain times it is difficult for any company to predict what could disrupt their business. Could any of us have predicted COVID?' asks Dinaz.

'No,' someone shouts.

'Can anyone predict where the next threat to humanity will come from and when?'

'No,' some employees shout in unison.

'Yet, an organisation needs to be ready to survive these threats. In my opinion, to do so, it needs to have a lean structure with fewer layers, a collaborative culture across functions and empowerment of people at the junior levels. This will allow them to huddle quickly if and when disaster strikes, take important decisions and kick off the execution process in a short span of time. So, how many hierarchical bands and sub-bands do we have at WeSolve?'

'Six bands and another seven sub-bands,' says the HR head.

'Isn't that a lot? Is that why we have designations like senior assistant deputy general manager? Why do you think we need so many bands?'

'People need to be promoted frequently to stay motivated,' someone adds.

'If I were to ask you to recall a couple of moments in your career when you felt the happiest, would these be the days that you got promoted or would they be occasions when your manager told you that he appreciated your handling of your people or your customers or the day he informed you, say, that he's increasing the size of your team or your territory? I'm willing to bet that for most of you, it would be the latter two and not the promotion that made you happier and for longer.'

Dinaz notices vigorous nods and smiles across the room.

She continues, 'What if we reduce the number of bands, increase responsibilities at each level so that every role is richer than what it is today? And if we have less mouths to feed, everyone gets to eat more too. Hence, I'm not saying that we pay the same for handling more responsibilities. Pay must also go up with responsibilities.'

The nods get even more vigorous.

'What if we empower people to take decisions without having to consult their seniors for every little activity? Do you think that would help motivate them and make up for the lack of a promotion every two years? And, why don't we increase the reward gap between high performers and others? I believe, right now, there isn't a great difference between someone who's rated "Outstanding" and another who's rated "Good".'

'That sounds like music to my ears. Undifferentiated rewards are a recipe for demotivating high performers and the single largest reason for their resignations. Let's work on this,' says the HR head.

'I also believe that people who collaborate are more optimistic and less cynical. I remember reading about a research study carried out in two fishing villages somewhere in Europe. While one village was near the sea, the other was by a lake. The people living close to the sea would go fishing on large motorised boats. They would work together as team for days on the boat and bring back a very large catch after a week at sea. They would consume a part of it themselves and sell most of the catch. In contrast, the fishermen who lived near the lake would go out fishing in small boats by themselves and compete on who caught the most fish. Each fisherman would carry a small load back every evening, just about enough to feed their family. The study revealed that the fishermen who fished in the sea and worked together had a more optimistic outlook. They were also richer than their fellow fishermen who fished in the lake. The latter, who competed with each other, were cynical about their own and the world's future.'

'How about we introduce free seating to promote collaboration between the different teams? On a day I'm working with a person from another team, I would like to sit next to them for that day. It would make my life much easier,' adds an employee.

'Nah! They tried that in my wife's company. It didn't work and led to discomfort and unhappiness amongst the employees,' says the HR head.

'Did everyone, including the senior leaders, move out of their cabins in your wife's company or was free seating only introduced for middle and junior management?' asks Dinaz.

'How could they have asked the VPs to sit out in the open? They've had their cabins and rooms for years.'

'What if we convert our office into an open-plan office where those of us who usually sit in cabins, too, come out and sit with everyone else? This would obviously include me,' suggests Dinaz.

'Is that even possible?'

'Why not? We can try and then see how that goes.'

'Now moving on to the next point. If our aim is really to empower our employees, then should they not be measured by what they deliver and how efficient they are instead of the number of hours they spend at work?' asks Dinaz.

'That'd be so cool,' an employee pipes in.

'So we can consider doing away with marking attendance and let people decide where they want to work from—office or home or someplace else—with a caveat that it should not affect their efficiency or their ability to deliver on their objectives.'

'Wow! Won't people misuse this facility?' asks the HR head.

'I've realised that we can never know what our employees do on their laptops when they are at work. At the end of the day, we are still relying on their ability to deliver on their work. If they are able to do so while working from outside of the office, why not just let them do it? It would at least save our employees the time they spend in the commute, which they could then use for spending quality time with their families.'

'What you say makes a lot of sense, Dinaz! Let's give it some more thought. I have another concern though. How do we segregate the drivers and the passengers when it comes to our projects? When people work in teams, there are a few who carry the load while others do minimal work. Yet, when at the end of the day, the group's performance is assessed, everyone in the group is given equal credit. Think of it this way. Twenty people are supposed to be pulling on a rope tied to a weight. But only a few people do the actual pulling while most just hold on to the rope and pretend to pull. Then why should the credit for pulling the rope go to those who did nothing. I think this really demoralises people,' says the HR head.

'Interesting analogy. Why don't you work with your team and come up with a way to identify individual accountabilities, even where people are working in groups. The final appraisal of any employee can be the weighted average of their individual contribution plus their group's performance,' suggests Dinaz.

For the next two hours, questions and answers fly back and forth between Dinaz and WeSolve's employees. She is happy to see that once the meeting is over, people walk out smiling and engaging in animated conversations with their colleagues. There is a look of surprise on the faces of her direct reportees at the success of the meeting. It's like they cannot believe what just happened and what they just heard.

In her next meeting with just the HR head, Dinaz suggests that it would be better for them to engage an external consultant who will review the existing bands, suggest reductions, review the goal-setting process and the joint accountabilities. The HR head agrees with Dinaz, feeling that her team might not be able to objectively evaluate something they have themselves created. So, an external person will help.

The office administration team invites bids from interior designers to carve out a large open and free seating space, while converting what is now offices into meeting rooms. This will allow the employees to experiment with a kind of an open-plan office without making too many structural changes. If it works, the company can consider completely doing away with cabins.

The other suggestion to have people put up stories of collaboration, experimentation and ownership by the people around them on the intranet is also coming about well. Dinaz, too, uses the platform to commend the HR head for collaborating with her colleagues and successfully aligning WeSolve's employees with the new organisation structure and appraisal process. At the end of the quarter, from all the entries received, twenty people are selected from across the country to spend a day with Dinaz.

On the meet-the-CEO day, the selected people are

transported to the head office in Shoreditch from across the country. Some are flying on an airplane for the first time in their lives and are very excited to meet the CEO. Dinaz spends the first hour of the day talking to people and asking them to explain what business they think WeSolve is in. Most people say fintech, or some version of that. Once they are done, Dinaz speaks up and says, 'Actually, our job is to remove any difficulties that our customers face, and to find ways for them to stay focused on their business and grow it. We are not a tech business. Technology only enables us.'

She also asks the select group to tell her in their own words the reason for them getting selected over their other colleagues. She makes notes while people speak. She plans to email a summary of the discussion to everyone in the company, in the hope that it will encourage others to start engaging in CEO activities too.

Finally, she asks everyone to talk about the things in WeSolve that, as per them, aren't working in the way they should. Some people talk about the quality of toilets, others about the choice of food in the cafeteria, etc. After a while, Dinaz deliberately steers the conversation towards work by asking for their suggestions on how else WeSolve can make the lives of its customers easier. What follows is a long list of ideas that reaffirms her belief that it is the people at the front end of an organisation who are the closest to the customers and their problems. The big takeaway from this is that all that managers needed to do was to talk with the people working at the frontlines instead of debating issues endlessly in meeting rooms.

At the end of the day, most attendees approach Dinaz to speak to her or to take a picture with her, to which she happily obliges. Later at home, she realises that she has received multiple alerts from various social media sites where the pictures clicked that day have been posted. It pleases her to see the enthusiasm of the people she met.

A couple of days later, she speaks with WeSolve's regional managers to find out about the reactions of those people who attended the meet-the-CEO event. One RM sums it up by saying, 'The two people from my region who attended the meeting with you were mobbed in the office on the morning after their return. Their colleagues wanted to know everything that had transpired at the meeting. I can now see those who weren't selected trying out new things that could get them a seat at the next meeting.' Dinaz is also told that the attendees gleefully told their colleagues about everything they discussed with her. It is clear her conversations with the select group have provided great clarity on what WeSolve's role ought to be in the life of its customers.

A week later, Dinaz writes another mail to everyone:

> Dear CEOs,
>
> There are many things around us that we would like to change. There are many opportunities that can make the lives of our customers and colleagues much easier. Yet, we are so engrossed with our daily jobs that we almost never think about how we can resolve them.

> I am inviting each one of you to think of one or two such things and write to me about it.
>
> Once I have all your mails, I'll select forty ideas that I find critical and useful and invite you to head/be a part of a CEO project that will aim to solve the problem highlighted by you. You will be allowed to form your own four-member cross-functional team to find a solution to these problems with a finite end date. I, along with my leadership team colleagues, will be reviewing ten projects at a time once a week to figure out progress and to see if you require any help, financial or otherwise, to complete your project. By the end of the month, every project will have been reviewed by me and my colleagues.
>
> Finally, the leadership team will rank the projects after considering their uniqueness, collaborative efforts of the project team and the size of the impact they could have on the lives of our customers. The top three project teams will be rewarded 5,000, 3,000 and 1,000 pounds, respectively.
>
> So, look around, find an area that you think deserves attention and a solution, type out the problem statement and mail it to me, now.
>
> I'm waiting.
>
> Best,
> Dinaz

She receives 246 mails in the next three days and as promised, she selects forty entries and allows the project management team to run the process thereafter.

At the next board review, the chairman of the board

commends the HR head for almost halving WeSolve's attrition rate in the last two years. Another director points out that the attrition rate amongst employees with high ratings is almost half of the attrition rate of those with lower ratings. This is a complete reversal from the day when good performers would leave WeSolve due to lack of appreciation while low performers continued to stay.

Sometime later, when the processes set up by Dinaz are moving with full speed, she takes a day off to attend an F1 event at Silverstone. This is the first event at Silverstone since the onset of COVID-19, and for two seasons, Dinaz hasn't been able to attend the races, something she has sorely missed. To her surprise she finds Paul, her predecessor, sitting in the same arena.

Paul grabs her hand and shakes it vigorously as he says, 'Dinaz, you superwoman! What a pleasant surprise to see you here. I didn't know you followed F1 too. I have to congratulate you on your achievement. It's amazing! Who could've ever imagined that the WeSolve business could double its turnover in two years. It seems you have magical powers. Well done, my friend!'

Dinaz responded, 'I'm no magician, Paul. I just believe that people have good intentions and it is our job to create an environment that channels these intentions.'

Here are some statements that you should respond to for the business that you are a part of, as an owner or a manager. Remember to respond honestly.

The statements must be answered in a yes/no format. If there are any statements that are not relevant to your business, put a cross against them.

- ☐ We have identified and shared with our employees the human factors that drive growth for our business as well as the ones that facilitate it.
- ☐ We have identified at least three competencies that define our work culture.
- ☐ We have multiple programmes that create awareness of and boost these competencies, at every level of the organisation.
- ☐ People are rewarded or penalised for adherence or non-adherence to these competencies, and our appraisal and promotion process attaches a significant weightage to these.
- ☐ Our goal-setting and appraisal processes are designed to recognise individual effort.
- ☐ Less than 5 per cent of employees are awarded the highest rating and their reward is significantly higher than those rated lower. The highest rated employees are signed off at a joint meeting of the leadership team.
- ☐ We have five or less bands between the CEO and the customer-facing employees.
- ☐ Every band change means a change of role and responsibility.

- ☐ Employees in one band report only to someone in a higher band.
- ☐ The empowerment of our frontline is reviewed and enhanced every year.

Now consider the statements to which you have responded with a 'No'. Discuss and reflect on these within your company, read more about **organisation culture** and/or ask some experts about how to apply these statements to your specific case.

Doing this could help you discover your work culture and refresh it to help achieve your goals.

10

MORE THAN AN ASSEMBLY OF PARTS

Staying relevant and growing margins

'This is 2001, not 1985 when we were a poorer country. Thailand has had a couple of decades of unprecedented growth. Even though the last couple of years were tough, they're behind us now. Most people are rich, travel abroad and have been exposed to the best the world has to offer. We can't continue to sell the mechanical watches that we have been selling since 1985 anymore. Nobody wants them.'

Badin is arguing with his father Kantee, the founder of an indigenous watch-making factory that he started in 1985 from his backyard in the Map Ta Phut Industrial Estate in Rayong province of Thailand. Before this, Kantee used to run a small ancillary unit for a car assembly plant and supplied four of their smallest components, which he manufactured himself.

He did this for a long time, and the increasing sales of cars over the years gave a boost to his sales too.

In the early 1980s, Kantee read an article which said that a wristwatch contains at least 171 small parts, which could even go up to 3,000 parts in an expensive Swiss watch. Fascinated by the idea of assembling something from such small parts, he decided to try his hand at watch manufacturing. At first, he just explored the field by opening a few watches and separating their components to understand them. With every watch he dismantled, his curiosity kept growing until he had fully figured out the mechanism of a wristwatch. He realised that there were no locally manufactured watches in Thailand at that time.

By 1985, not only had he figured out the mechanism and components for the kind of watch he wanted to make but he had also found a company in Japan which was ready to supply him with a tool-cutting machine. On this machine, Kantee fabricated the 200-odd components of his first watch. He named his watch brand after his young daughter, Dara.

In the Thailand of the 1980s, there were hardly any locally manufactured brands, except for a few brands that sold fabrics and incense sticks. The country had become a good place for the assembly of international cars and other machine-based products because of the relatively cheap Thai labour. In such a climate, the government took a fancy to a Thai-made watch and granted special incentives to Kantee to help him promote his watch within Thailand and the rest of the world too.

Till the early 1990s, Dara watches sold very well in the

country through generic watch stores. Even though the Dara range of watches was almost 200-strong and suited international tastes, Kantee felt that the brand was getting lost amongst the numerous second-hand copies of international watch brands—coming to Thailand from China—that were flooding the generic watch stores in Thailand.

In 1991, Kantee decided to launch branded Dara stores that would only sell Dara watches. He franchised a store in every district with some rich provinces having as many as twenty stores. Within a few years, he had opened almost 300 stores across the country, making Dara the largest watch brand in South East Asia, based on the volume of watches sold.

Business boomed for the next ten years but by the turn of the century, volumes of watches sold started to taper. Some franchisees even shut down due to poor sales while others were threatening to follow suit.

This was the time when Kantee's son Badin, who had studied in a prestigious American university, came back and started questioning the viability of Dara. The conversations between Kantee and Badin, often heated, became a daily feature in their living room.

'Dad, you can't continue to sell your customers the same product you've been selling for decades. People get bored and they want something newer, fancier.'

'But people of this country have been buying my watches for over two decades now, and so far I have not received any complaints. And we keep introducing new models every now and then too. We also have three automatic watches for the youngsters who don't like winding their watch every day. What is there to be bored about? Haven't you heard the saying "old is gold"?'

'I'm not denying, Dad, that your watches are so good that they can last for more than a decade. They also don't lose or gain time even after ten years of wearing. But that also means that people have no reason to buy a new watch from us for a very long time. And if they do decide to change their watch for the novelty factor, they usually turn to a different brand altogether. In such a scenario, why wouldn't our sales stagnate?'

'So, what do you expect me to do, start making bad watches?' asks Kantee.

'Not at all, but we do need to rethink the business. Maybe add some more products to the business so that the sales don't stagnate any further. Otherwise our remaining franchisees will abandon us too.'

'Son, I don't know what you have in mind. But I suggest you first conduct some sort of a market survey or hire a company to do market research for you before making any changes to our business.'

Taking his father's advice, Badin goes around the markets, meets many customers, speaks to his friends too, till he realises something very basic. That night, after dinner, he discusses his idea with Kantee.

'Dad, I'm sure you know most people buy a watch to use it to keep time.'

'Yes, son, that's what a watch is supposed to do, isn't it?'

'Yes, it is. For a lot of people, it is a thing of necessity that serves a purpose. Just like a shoe protects your feet, a shirt covers your body, a pen helps you write, sunglasses protect your eyes. All these are items of necessity and for most people having only one piece of any of these items would suffice. Yet a lot of people have more than one pair of shoes, shirts, pens and sunglasses. Have you considered why that is so?'

'Because apart from performing the basic function that they're supposed to perform, these products have also become items of fashion as well as status symbols. They help a person express their personality. Some of these products even make people feel more confident than they actually are. I would say that the second shirt, the second pair of shoes, the second pen are all items of luxury instead of necessity.'

'Exactly my point. Why can't a watch become an item of luxury too? Why should we expect a person to own only one watch for their necessity? Why can't a person wear a watch as a fashion statement or a status symbol? If we accept that premise, then a person can have more than one watch, maybe a watch for each occasion. Maybe one for each dress they own? Just like their shoes, shirts, pens and sunglasses.'

'You have a thought there, Badin.'

'And do you know that over half of Thailand still does not wear a watch?' asks Badin.

'Yes, of course. A watch is an expensive item. Many

components are assembled together to create a watch, and each component is designed and fabricated to specification. Manufacturing watches costs money, which is why owning a watch is expensive.'

'Dad, I've been doing some research. Why don't we start manufacturing quartz watches? They don't have as many components, maybe a fourth of the components that a mechanical watch has. Quartz watches can be manufactured cheaply, hence they are more affordable. And with these quartz watches that are cheaper to manufacture, we can have more variety to help us sell multiple watches to our high-end customers. Maybe even at a higher margin.'

'Is this what they taught you in the US? You want me to start selling Casio watches now?'

'Dad, not even for a moment am I asking you to start competing with Casio. Their watches and their business model are different from ours. I know you love watches, but you are also someone who appreciates efficiency. Last week, you discarded your bicycle in favour of a motorbike. They are both machines but the latter is more efficient, so you decided to move forward with something more efficient. The same is true for watches.'

'But a mechanical watch is a piece of art; owning it is a pleasure and a privilege. A quartz watch can never be the same.'

'Dad, most of the world has by now accepted the quartz watch because it's cheaper and needs less maintenance and management. It also allows people to own multiple watches.

Imagine owning more than one mechanical watch and spending an hour every day, before going to sleep, winding all your watches. It sounds so tedious.'

'Badin, you are asking me to make a big change in my business model. I need some time to think about it.'

Over the next few days, Kantee gives Badin's words a lot of thought and eventually comes to terms with it. Even though he hates the idea of giving up his beautiful mechanical watches, his son's logic is too strong to ignore. He finally tells Badin that he is ready to give his idea a shot. While Kantee gets down to work on a plan for manufacturing quartz watches, Badin gets busy hiring and inducting designers who have worked in other fashion categories and are now creating a whole new range of fashion watches for Dara. He hires merchandisers who have worked in fashion retail to create show window designs for the new stores. He engages with communication agencies to come up with an advertising strategy that supports repositioning the watch as a fashion object.

The organisation is larger, with many new faces who have worked in other industries. Meeting rooms are abuzz with new ideas and teams are excited because they are creating a new brand while synthesising their learnings from across industries.

Working on a quartz watch is simpler, on one hand, because the number of components is much smaller than a mechanical watch. But it is more difficult at the same time because the components of a quartz watch are smaller, more delicate, hence working with them requires more precision. But Kantee's years of expertise with handling mechanical components come in handy, and he starts enjoying working with the new materials for the quartz watches. He experiments with different materials, trying to make the components thinner and lighter, and takes the thickness of the watch down to 1.5 mm and the weight to 50 grams, something that was unimaginable so far. The lightest watch that Kantee ever produced before weighed 85 grams. Quartz is a new frontier for him and he is happy to meet the challenge that has been put to him.

It is still Kantee who has the final word on what goes inside the Dara quartz watches, and it is he who deals with the manufacturing end of the business with the existing Dara team he has worked with for decades. Badin hires a few youngsters who are good at managing outsourced design and communication agencies. The young and the old challenge each other but still collaborate and coexist, because Kantee and Badin are aligned towards one single outcome, which is to make Dara as profitable as it was in the past.

Badin's discussions with the creative agencies on pitching a watch as a fashion accessory takes them in the direction of creating different designs of watches for home wear, office wear, evening wear and formal wear. It is a designer's delight to work on the different dial and case designs and combinations to suit all these occasions. They have also identified their different target segments like students, housewives, older people who need larger numerals and backlit screens in watches, amongst others. The designers start working on designs for each of these segments. The marketing and PR agencies are also looking into coming up with suitable names for the different watches being designed to suit different segments and occasions. There is a new upbeat energy at Dara which no one has ever seen before.

Kantee takes Badin to regional franchisee conferences with him where, after he has introduced Badin, he lets his son hold forth and explain what the new Dara brand is attempting. They also showcase some of the new models they are planning to launch along with their price points at these conferences.

There is a sense of optimism and euphoria amongst franchisee owners, and everyone signs up to renovate their shops before the launch date of the new watches. Some even want to move to a larger shop or open a new one to accommodate the new range and the increased footfall that they expect it to bring in. By the time father and son land in Phuket for the third franchisee meet, the word has spread and there are local business people as well as some from the neighbouring provinces who have gathered at the venue to meet the Dara team and seek future franchise opportunities.

The launch goes as expected. People rush to the stores to check out the new range. Sales are brisk. Kantee's decision to double the manufacturing capability and hold back exports for a couple of months is also paying off, because after all, retail sales within Thailand are more profitable as compared to bulk orders from overseas, where Dara has to compete with Chinese knock-off watches.

These winds of change carry Dara forward for the next ten years. The brand, as a practice, introduces almost 200 new models every year while withdrawing around a 100 to keep people's interest in Dara watches alive. By now Kantee's daughter, Dara, after whom the brand is named, has finished college and joined the business too. Her interest lies in design and that's what she has studied at college. She spends most of her time with the design team coming up with new models to introduce in the market. Having his son and daughter actively engaged in business, Kantee has taken a back seat and prefers to spend more and more of his time at home with Badin's children, a five-year-old boy and a three-year-old girl, who are both very fond of their grandfather.

One evening, Kantee brings up the subject of succession at the dinner table. He is clear that he wants to divide the business into two parts, one for each of his two children, before he retires. Badin and Dara are surprised at what Kantee has in mind. They protest, saying that there are still many years before he has to retire and that they are siblings who would be happy to run the business together even after Kantee retires. But Kantee ignores their protests and tells them that his decision has been prompted by the many stories he has heard of squabbles between siblings that have destroyed the value of a business built over decades in a matter of a few years. He explains that while things may look hunky-dory now, the arrival of Dara's husband and children in the picture and with Badin's children growing up, the pie will need to be divided one day. So why not do it now?

He concludes the conversation by saying, 'You have five years to build another business together which one of you can inherit while the other inherits the Dara business. Or, you could split the Dara business into two regions, North and South Thailand, and run them as two distinct businesses. It's all up to the two of you. Research, discuss, do whatever, but let me know in three months what you've decided, so that we can get cracking on whichever path you choose.'

Things have been smooth between brother and sister, who have worked together for years in Dara. Badin is also very fond of his sister, who is eight years younger to him, and it is difficult for him to even contemplate a split with her. But they both appreciate their father's foresight and the long rope he's given them to think and plan leisurely and amicably, instead of doing it with the help of lawyers down the line, acrimoniously.

They spend a lot of time discussing the ideas that Kantee has thrown their way.

'We could simply find ways to sell more watches just like we did earlier. That's what we do best,' says Dara.

'Well, Dara, the market for watches is of a particular size and even if we have convinced people in the past to buy more than one watch, there will come a time when people will run out of wrists and occasions for which to buy a watch. At the time, all we'll be left with would be replacement demand, to replenish the watches they've misplaced or lost interest in. Even the population growth has slowed down, so the rate at which new watch wearers appear in the market is also very slow. I don't think just selling more watches is a solution for what Dad is suggesting. Even if we decide to split the Dara business between the north and south regions of Thailand, all we'll be doing is competing with each other, which won't be very good for either of us in the long run.'

'Then how do we look for and set up a new business about which we know nothing? At least, we have over two decades of watch-making expertise.'

'What you say is interesting Dara. Do you think watch-making is our expertise?'

'Isn't it?' asks Dara.

'That's the product we sell. But what skills have we built in the process of selling watches that can help us build a new business?'

'We understand customer needs,' suggest Dara.

'Someone who sells cookies understands that too.'

'OK, let me put it differently. We understand their fashion needs.'

'And what can we do with that skill?' asks Badin.

'We can use that understanding to create designs for other products that fall in the category of fashion. And we also have the requisite retailing skills. We know how to drive customers to our stores and merchandise our products in a manner that tempts them to buy them.'

'Excellent! So, I think what we should start with is looking for other products that are a part of an individual's fashion needs and explore the idea of manufacturing and selling them. What products can you think of off the top of your head?'

'Clothes, shoes, sunglasses, perfumes. I think if we just walk around the Central World Mall in Bangkok, we'll find all our answers.'

'This list would give us an idea of what customers want to buy to meet their fashion needs. The thing you and I are good at is creating tempting propositions for our customers. Now let's look at what manufacturing skills we have and which of these fashion products can be made using our existing skill set.'

'We make watches. Can't we make a shirt or a perfume using the same manufacturing skills?' asks Dara.

'What is the core skill required to make watches?'

'Dad was very good at one time in manufacturing those small components that are assembled to make a watch. We used to manufacture and assemble 200 small pieces to make a mechanical watch. Now we make fifty of those small pieces, put them together and voila, we have a watch.'

'Is there a fashion product you can think of that can be deconstructed into small components, which can be assembled after manufacture?'

'I studied jewellery design at college and remember my teacher saying that any piece of jewellery can be made from eight to ten basic components like balls, wires, etc. Maybe there is something there for us. After all, jewellery is also a part of fashion. Isn't it?'

'Yes, it is. But it involves precious metals and it is made one piece at a time, that too by hand, which is painfully slow. We need something that can be scaled up,' says Badin.

'Not all jewellery is made of gold, rubies and precious gems. Just like clothes and watches, jewellery, too, can be broken into different categories for day, evening and occasion wear. Have a look at the jewellery I wear and you'll notice that. Just like only 5 per cent of watches we make in Dara have a gold case, only 10 per cent of my jewellery is made of gold.'

'Is that true? I never knew that. Maybe we have something there. It's worth exploring, Dara.'

That is the beginning of a longer conversation, which is followed by months of market research and exploration, which culminates in them launching a jewellery brand in Thailand called Lakha, which means 'precious' in Thai.

Together they identify new skills that the watch business does not have but the jewellery business requires and hire people from other industries to fill the gap, just as they did when they scaled up the watch business after they replaced mechanical technology with quartz.

Five years later, Badin and Dara have two successful brands in Thailand, each growing fast. Badin runs Dara, the watch brand which sells basic time-keeping devices to the masses while fulfilling the fashion needs of his premium customers who want to own a different Dara watch for different occasions of their lives.

His sister Dara, on the other hand, runs Lakha, the jewellery brand. When she was starting out, Kantee helped her create the manufacturing facilities she needed and transferred over a couple of his trusted employees from the watch factories to handle the jewellery factories and supply chain functions. Dara manages the design, merchandising and retailing parts of the business and has created different sub-brands that cater to different occasions and different needs, such as artificial jewellery for day wear, semi-precious jewellery for evening wear and gold jewellery for occasion wear.

Kantee has retired by now and plays golf five days a week, something he has always wanted to do.

The growth of the business and margins are what have kept his mind busy, and he thinks about this often between holes on the golf course, trying to think of new challenges to throw at his children to ensure they adapt to changing circumstances.

Here are some statements that you should respond to for the business that you are a part of, as an owner or a manager. Remember to respond honestly.

The statements must be answered in a yes/no format. If there are any statements that are not relevant to your business, put a cross against them.

- ☐ At least one of our current strategic priorities deals with a new customer segment or customer need.
- ☐ Our strategy team creates a rolling five-year plan that captures customers' needs and technology options.

- ☐ As much as 20 per cent of our current revenues come from products that did not exist and from customer segments we did not cater to three years ago.
- ☐ As much as 40 per cent of our new hires in the last one year are from industries other than ours.
- ☐ There is a trained and dedicated project management team in place to track and guide the top ten projects at any given time.
- ☐ In the last year, none of our innovation projects has been delayed or abandoned.
- ☐ We have a widely known, ongoing innovation suggestion programme with monetary rewards.
- ☐ Once every quarter, our operations team benchmarks our practices with those of other industries to identify non-linear change opportunities.
- ☐ In the last year, we have changed the delivery model of at least one activity that contributes to more than 1 per cent of the total cost or revenue.
- ☐ As much as 40 per cent of our senior leadership team has worked in other countries, functions and industries.

Now consider the statements to which you have responded with a 'No'. Discuss and reflect on these within your company, read more about **innovation** and/or ask some experts about how to apply these statements to your specific case.

Doing this could help you reinvent your business whenever signs of stagnation start surfacing.

www.ingramcontent.com/pod-product-compliance
Lightning Source LLC
Chambersburg PA
CBHW062114160726
48282CB00026B/794
* 9 7 8 9 3 6 0 4 5 2 6 1 2 *